# TAUN . . .

# ITS HISTORY

AND

# MARKET TRUST



BY

GEORGE H. KITE & H. P. PALMER.

---

Si Monumentum Requiris, Circumspice.

# LIST OF ILLUSTRATIONS.

# TAUNTON:

## ITS HISTORY AND MARKET TRUST.

### CHAPTER I.

TAUNTON NOT A ROMAN BUT A SAXON TOWN—FOUNDATION BY KING INA—DESTRUCTION—REBUILT—BURNT BY THE DANES—AGAIN REBUILT—A "BOROUGH," POSSESSING A MINT AND A MARKET—ITS HISTORY TO REIGN OF STEPHEN.

THE district in which Taunton lies was from very early days in the hands of the Britons. After the Roman conquest, it was under the dominion of the Romans.

It was formerly believed by archæologists that Taunton existed in Roman times, but this belief is now definitely abandoned. No such relics have been found here as would have been discovered had this been the case. Such Roman remains as have been unearthed suffice only to prove that the Romans were in occupation of the district, in the same sense that they occupied the whole country. The inhabitants of the district during this period of Roman rule were, as before, the Britons, who had to obey the Roman military rule. When the Romans left the country, the district was again under the undisputed sway of the Britons.

The Saxon invasion soon followed the departure of the Romans, but it was many years before the land in which Taunton lies was subdued. In 600, only a small part of Somerset was conquered. By 700, the conquest had extended as far as W. Monkton. The Anglo-Saxon tribe which thus conquered Somerset was known as the Sumorsetæ, who have given their name to Somerset as well as to Somerton, once the principal town.

The conquest of the greater part of Somerset was effected by Cenwealh and his successor, Ina, who came to the throne in 688.

Ina, King of Wessex, in 710, anxious to protect his conquests from the Britons or Welsh of Devon, built probably of earth and timber, on the site of Taunton Castle, a fortress, known as Taunton—the "tun" or dwelling on the "ton," that is, on the "water."

Such was the beginning of Taunton, and Ina, and no one else, was the founder of Taunton. As Freeman says, "Taunton was no doubt built as a fortress on the frontier to guard the newly conquered land against the Welshmen in Devon."

The Taunton, thus founded by Ina, was only born to be destroyed. In 722, the King's cousin, Ealdbryt, claimed the throne of Wessex. He was acting, we may well believe, in collusion with the Welsh. He succeeded in procuring admission into the Castle and held it against Ina. He was ignominiously ejected by Ethelburga, Ina's Queen, and the fortress burnt to the ground. Taunton seems to have been rebuilt not long after these events, either by Ina or his successor, Ethelard. In the reign of the latter, it became the centre of the great Manor of Taunton, given by the King and Frithogytha, his wife, to the Bishop of Winchester. The memory of the rule of the Bishops is still perpetuated in the

" Winchester Arms," lying on ground once occupied by some of the buildings belonging to the Bishop.

These Prince-Bishops, for such they really were, ruled the Manor for many ages.

In 1001, Taunton was burnt to the ground by the Danes. Domesday Book, however, shows very plainly that it must have been rebuilt and become a very flourishing town in the reign of Edward the Confessor. It was able to pay the Bishop a handsome annual revenue.

We see then that Taunton has been built or rebuilt no less than three times.

In Saxon, as in Norman, days it possessed " borough right." It was in the old sense of the term a " borough," which meant a town defended by military burgesses, of whom in William I.'s time there were 64.

It possessed a mint and coined its own money. Above all, it had a market, one of the great gifts conferred on the town by Edward the Elder. As cattle and goods of any kind could only be sold in a Market, this gift must have added immensely to the prosperity of the town, and brought in buyers and sellers from the whole country-side.

The Rev. D. P. Alford, in his " History of Taunton Castle," disputes the current belief that the substantial Norman Castle, which was built in early Norman times, was the work of William Giffard, who founded the Priory. The building of the Norman Keep is assigned by Mr. Alford to the succeeding Bishop of Winchester, Henry of Blois, brother of King Stephen.

## CHAPTER II.

Warbeck's Rebellion—Henry VII. at Taunton—The Town Holds Out Against Charles I.—Smollett's Description of Taunton in 1769—A Corporation Granted and Taken Away—The Second Corporation, How Lost—The Third Corporation—The Duke of Monmouth—Politics of the Town.

IN 1495, in the reign of Henry VII., the Castle was repaired by William Langton, then Bishop of Winchester and Lord of the Manor. The Bishop added the gateway facing Castle Green, which bears his escutcheon as well as the arms of Henry VII. In 1497, the town and castle were seized, after his failure to storm Exeter, by Perkin Warbeck, one of the two pretenders in Henry's reign. Warbeck had been proclaimed as King Richard IV. in Cornwall, and he came to Taunton accompanied by disaffected Cornishmen. Finding himself closely pursued by the Earl of Devon, and knowing that Henry was also advancing against him, Warbeck left his followers, went to Beaulieu, and took sanctuary there. Henry arrived in Taunton to find he had no enemy to fight. While here, he stayed at the Priory, as the Castle was still in the hands of the masons.

In the earlier part of the Great Civil War, Somerset was held for the King. The great exception was Taunton, which was captured by the Parliament in 1642. Lost to the Parliament in 1643, it was won back by Blake in 1644. Attacked by the royalist troops under Goring in 1645, it was brilliantly defended by Blake.

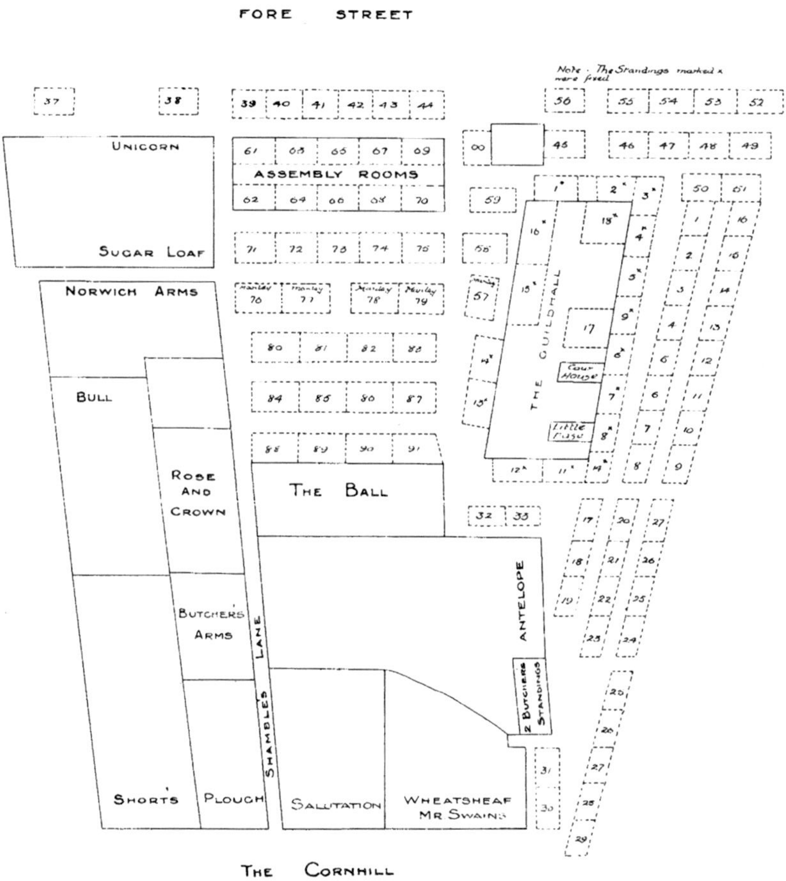


PLAN OF CENTRE OF TAUNTON, 1768,

*Copied by Mr. H. C. Charlewood from old plan in the possession of Mr. E. E. Baker.*

This great Somerset soldier held the town until a portion of the force under Lord Fairfax was detached for its relief, and under the command of Colonel Weldon, raised the seige.

Writing in 1769, early in the reign of George III., Tobias Smollett, the historian and novelist, places the population of Taunton at the large figure of 20,000. This number seems to be based on a return made in the reign of William and Mary, and perpetuated afterwards. The estimate is erroneous. Basing his calculations on the returns of the number of householders by the tithing-men, in 1703, Mr. H. Byard Sheppard has shown that the population of Taunton at that time was about 3,880. In 1851 it had increased to 14,176, and in 1926 it is estimated to be 25,000. Smollett, after giving such a misleading statement of the population of Taunton, tells us that the Tone, in 1769, was navigable from Taunton to Bridgwater. It was spanned by a bridge of six arches.

Smollett describes the streets of Taunton as "spacious and clean." Strangers visiting the town, however, were somewhat repelled by the smell of the oil, which was used in the woollen manufactories here. In those days, Taunton was the centre of a large manufacture of woollen goods. Smollett was struck by the Puritanism of the town, of which we still have remains in the excision of "Saint" from Mary Street and Paul Street, while, in Cromwell's Protectorate, the two parishes of the town were known as "Magdalene" and "James." The Puritans often called themselves "the saints" or "the elect." It is difficult to explain why they denied the former title to the Apostles and others. All the Nonconformist denominations, according to Smollett's statement, had meeting-houses in the town. He undoubtedly refers to Paul's Meeting, the Unitarian Chapel, then possessed by the Baptists, and the Quakers' Meeting-place, in Bath Place. Of these three buildings only one survives, as he knew it. Paul's Meeting and the Quakers' Chapel have been rebuilt, but the Unitarian Chapel remains as it was in his time.* Smollett mentions an Academy designed to train candidates for the Nonconformist Ministry. He alludes to two Churches, St. Mary's and St. James', several Almshouses and what he describes as "a well endowed Free School," by which he means Bishop Fox's Grammar School, which was conducted in the present Municipal Buildings until 1870. The Assizes were held in the great Hall of the Castle.

It has been stated that Taunton was the centre of a great ecclesiastical Manor belonging to the Bishop of Winchester. Towns belonging to ecclesiastical Manors were, as a rule, the last to receive the benefit of local government, and the frequent failure of the clergy, especially the monastic bodies, to surrender any of their rights was one among the many causes which brought about the Peasants' Revolt, in 1381. It is hardly credible that with the exception of the Saxon borough-court no form of local government beyond the antique one of the Court Leet existed in Taunton till 1627. It was then for the first time that the civil power passed into the hands of a Mayor, Aldermen and

* It is interesting to note that no less a person than the poet Coleridge has stood in the pulpit of that Chapel.

Burgesses. The fact that Taunton had resisted the King in the Civil War was not forgotten at the accession of Charles II. The town walls were destroyed and the charter forfeited. The town, however, found later a good friend in Dr. Peter Mew, then Bishop of Bath & Wells, a veteran of the Civil War, who had exchanged the sword for the cassock. Mew, some years later, when Bishop of Winchester, lent his horses to Feversham, to drag the royal guns into position at the battle of Sedgemoor.

Mew interceded with Charles II., and prevailed on him to grant a new charter to Taunton.

At the time when Smollett wrote, in 1769, the Corporation consisted of a Mayor, Richard Manning, a Recorder, a Justice, two Aldermen, 24 Capital Burgesses, a Town Clerk, two Constables, two Portreeves, and two Sergeants at Mace. Smollett tells us that the Corporation possessed "no lands or houses or store of money, and the Mayor very trifling privileges, in comparison of those of other places." He represents the town as flourishing, the Corporation as "the poorest in the county." This Corporation, as described by Smollett, existed until 1792, when neglect to fill vacancies brought about its dissolution.

Taunton was again without a charter. It remained shorn of its privileges until 1877, when a fresh charter was granted.

The Duke of Monmouth had been well known in the neighbourhood in the reign of Charles II., and been greeted with royal honours by thousands of people. It is no wonder therefore that he was most warmly wellcomed in Taunton when he staked his all in a trial of strength against James II. Tauntonians had to deplore the execution of the Duke as well as of prominent citizens of the town. It is not surprising that the inhabitants, as Smollett says, "were among the first to join the Prince of Orange on his landing." They still remained, in Smollett's days, zealous and determined Whigs.

## CHAPTER III.

TAUNTON, ONCE A SAXON AND NORMAN "BOROUGH," BECOMES A REPRESENTATIVE "BOROUGH"—SOME EMINENT REPRESENTATIVES—ELECTION PETITIONS—A TRIUMPH CELEBRATED AT THE MARKET HOUSE—THE SAXON AND EARLY NORMAN MARKET—ANCIENT TRADE AND MUNICIPAL MANAGEMENT—GILDS AND COURT LEET.

IT has already been stated that so long ago as the reign of Edward the Elder, the gifted son and successor of King Alfred, Taunton was a "borough." No such sense as is now borne by that term was implied then or for centuries afterwards. What was rather meant was that it was marked out from towns which had not "borough-right" by its possession of a borough-court, a market and a mint. In a word, it became the important town, the business centre, as we say, of the district.

Places which appear as "boroughs" in Saxon and Norman times were among those selected to send members to Parliament, when the idea of representative government was evolved.

Taunton was among the earliest towns to return members to Parliament, and then became a "borough," as we understand that term.

It was in the year 1295, that Edward I. summoned what is known as "the Model Parliament," and to that Parliament Taunton sent two representatives. In the reign of Queen Elizabeth, one of the borough members for two years was Francis Bacon, probably the greatest man of his age, except Shakespeare. Sir Francis Warre, of Hestercombe, was one of the members during the whole of the reign of Queen Anne, and Sir Benjamin Hammet from 1784 to 1800, the date of his decease.

Smollett makes special mention of the "potwallopers," or "potwallers." It seems that any man residing in Taunton, whether householder or lodger, and who really had "a settlement" in the town and was not a casual or stray from another district, and who, as Smollett puts it, "dressed his own victuals," could vote at an election. The history of Taunton from the beginning of the eighteenth century has been fruitful in election petitions, formerly decided by Committees of the House of Commons. On more than one occasion, the elections were pronounced void.

In 1775, for example, the defeated candidates of the election of October, 1774, were declared elected.

Soon afterwards they entered the town in triumph, accompanied by their supporters. The procession was magnificent. A cavalcade of nearly a thousand horsemen and many coaches proceeded through the town. They dismounted at the end of the Parade, and passed under a triumphal arch to the market-house. They then feasted in the "Assembly-room," and it may be conjectured that some of them, in the language of the day, were "merry." A ball followed in the evening, and the town blazed with a general illumination.

The Parade along which these joyous politicians passed, attended by the beauty and fashion of the district, the Market-house in which they feasted, the

Assembly-rooms in which the dance was held, were all new features in Taunton. We have now to see how the town was formerly governed, then will be shown the evils from which it had been delivered and the advantages which it had gained by the local patriotism and generosity to which the Market Trust owed its existence. Now when the Market Trustees have given, or are giving up, their stewardship, we shall have one more opportunity of contrasting the past with the present—one more chance of correcting the fallacy about "good old times." We shall see how those whose watchword was progress removed from the town some of the blots which disfigured it and made it more worthy of its history. It will not be questioned, moreover, that the town owes a great debt to the successive generations of Market Trustees who have faithfully discharged their duties for considerably over a century and a half.

We have seen that to Edward the Elder is ascribed the gift of a market to Taunton. Such a market would have been supervised by the portreeve of the town. There were no shops in these early days, and those in want of goods would make their way to the market. There can be little doubt the market at Taunton occupied the site of the existing Fore Street and Cheapside, which are so called because they were the seat of the market. Part of the ancient market may have covered, and probably did cover, the existing Parade. There, on stalls resembling those now seen on Saturdays on the Parade, was shown in Saxon and early Norman times every kind of merchandise, from country produce to musical instruments and choice wares from the Continent. Tolls were exacted both on goods coming into the town and on articles when sold, and such tolls were the perquisite of the Lord of the Manor, the Bishop of Winchester. The burgesses, who were once placed here by the Bishop to guard the town and repair the Castle and town walls, were gradually displaced by burgesses engaged in trade.

Gilds of traders became more prominent and regulated their trades. Charters of Incorporation no doubt lessened the powers of the Lord of the Manor over the Borough. Such powers as remained were the right of rent for setting up stalls in the market, dues and customs from certain trades, "rents and fines" from the Mills, and rent for land "in the lord's waste." So long as these payments were made, the Bishop had no longer control over the fortunes and business of the community.

We shall probably be correct in assuming that from the time of Henry III., and possibly before, the Gilds and the Court Leet conducted the municipal and judicial work of the town. The Gilds made the trade rules which were, to a certain extent, checked by the Court Leet in its attempt to enforce reasonable prices, at all events in the matter of provisions. The Court Leet, as Mr. B. Sheppard has pointed out, was the ultimate controlling authority. It possessed the powers now exercised by the Borough Magistrates, those enjoyed by the Mayor and Corporation, and those in the hands of the Market Trustees. It appointed the Police. It named the Tithing-men, or Aldermen. It was the Board of Guardians to the extent at any rate of dealing with "casuals," who, if they could be classed as "sturdy vagabonds," were placed not in a "workhouse," but in the stocks or pillory. It appointed the Portreeves, now, as the town had become more prosperous, increased to two. These Portreeves collected the rents due to the Bishop, and granted leases of standings or stalls in the market.

It is thus that the town must have been governed until it received its charter from Charles I. in 1627.

## CHAPTER IV.

COURT LEET STILL A POWER AFTER FIRST CHARTER—AGAIN THE PRINCIPAL AUTHORITY AFTER ITS FORFEITURE. INSTANCES OF ITS ACTION—DEFECTIVE SANITARY CONDITIONS OF FORMER DAYS—CONGESTION OF MARKETS—FORMER TAUNTON MARKET—THE MARKET CROSS—THE GUILDHALL—ANCIENT TOWN CELLS—CROWDING OF MARKET AREA—ELEVEN INNS ON THE SITE—BAD LIGHTING OF THE TOWN.

TO what extent the charter given to the town by Charles I. in 1627 superseded the authority of the Court Leet is difficult to determine. For some years, at all events, it would seem to have pursued the even tenor of its way and discharged its usual necessary, but hardly exciting, duties. We are, however, by no means without guidance in this matter. We find from Mr. Byard Sheppard's "Courts Leet and the Court Leet of the Borough of Taunton," that for some time after the charter was granted, it was the Court Leet which was still fixing the hours of the Yarn Market. It was taking steps to prevent the crowding of the Market on market days. Bakers who ventured to place ricks of broom, used for heating their ovens, too near their bakeries were ordered to remove them under penalties. The Court Leet had to listen to stories of "encroachments of a wall in Paul Street, a garden in Paul Street, and several encroachments into the Town Rhine." Such cases are sufficient to show that, charter or no charter, the Court Leet was not an extinct volcano, but remained very much in action. From 1639 to 1649 however, there was a slackening of energy. During that period, says Mr. Sheppard, "there are no petitions or presentments of nuisances recorded in the minute-books." The truth apparently is that the Civil War and the political turmoil immediately preceding it laid a paralysing clutch on ordinary civil life. Undoubtedly too, as Mr. Sheppard points out, the new Corporation may at last have been dealing with some of the duties hitherto discharged by the Court Leet.

In 1648, the rights still possessed over the Borough by the Bishop of Winchester, which included "ancient rents of the annual value of £24 2s. 2d.," were sold by the Parliament to two private individuals. The Bishops were regarded with peculiar enmity by the new government. They were summarily ejected, lost their revenues and were forced to hide their diminished heads in private life. Thus it came to pass, that for the first time since Saxon days, both the Borough and Manor of Taunton passed from the hands of the Bishop of Winchester. To whatever extent the Corporation was now discharging its duties, we find that during the Cromwellian supremacy the Court Leet was still the sanitary authority in the town. Offenders were brought before it "for throwing of sudds into the street," "not repairing the way which is defective before their doors," "stopping up the ancient rhine flowing from Pool Wall Mills to the River Tone," and maintaining nuisances on their premises.

In 1660, came the tide of reaction which brought Charles II. to the throne. The Bishop of Winchester recovered his rights over the Manor and the Borough. The resistance which Taunton had made to the royal forces in the Civil War and the Puritan reputation of the town lost it its charter. Once more it was entirely under the civic control of the Court Leet, and thus it remained till the granting of its second charter, in 1677. After that time, says Mr. Sheppard, "there are fewer presentments except in connection with the rhines and markets." It cannot be too clearly realised that our ancestors' ideas of sanitation were as far sundered from our own as one pole from the other. Their minds never roamed beyond the faintest obedience to the most elementary rules of public health and comfort. They were satisfied if a few glaring and obtrusive nuisances were corrected. They were not disposed, for example, to allow swine to ramble untended about the streets. They entertained the strongest objection to being bitten by uncontrolled "mastiff dogs," and called upon the town authorities to abate such a peril and nuisance. They drew the line at dunghills lying in the streets. They did more than protest when the offensive "rhines" which ran through the town, bearing to the river a horrid burden of sewage and refuse, were rendered unendurable by being blocked in their course. Neither in Taunton, nor in any other English town, were sanitary measures formerly anything more than the crudest attempts to banish evils, the mere possibility of which would scarcely suggest itself to ourselves. Unsuppressed nuisances indeed were the curse of every English town for centuries. Want of drainage, the pollution of wells, overcrowding, the absence of efficient scavenging, and the unclean habits of the people made such places the nests of every virulent disorder. Markets too were usually held near a densely populated area, where fevers and small-pox often ran riot. The result can only have been to carry further and further the seeds of disease and infect the healthier country people who came to the Market.

In the earlier days of the Middle Ages, when towns were smaller and when Markets were held in really open spaces, far better sanitary conditions prevailed than later. As the ages advanced, towns, as they grew larger, became not less, but more pestiferous. Markets became more and more a peril to the health of the community.

The ancient Taunton Market was held on the same site for centuries. To the same frequented piece of ground had come Saxons and Normans, the subjects of the Plantagenet, Lancastrian, Yorkist, Tudor, and Stuart dynasties. Changes there were round the seat of the Market. Houses covering the area now occupied by Fore Street and Cheapside had been erected there possibly soon after the Conquest. They encircled the Market just as we see them now round the Markets of many Continental towns. The Market area itself in Taunton was thus at length restricted to spaces the larger of which was known as "the Island" and the smaller "Cornhill." The "Island" was triangular, and perhaps so called because, along its sides, ran the "rhines" of the town. The "Cornhill," the part of the Market where corn was bought and sold, was on the site of the existing cross. On one side of the Cornhill was a Bull-ring; on the other, two mountebank stages. At the East end of the Market were the "shambles" or butchers' stalls, and we can imagine how they were kept in days when supervision was so inadequate. Near the entrance of the Market, not far from the White Hart

Inn, stood the Market Cross.* This cross, built late in the 15th or early in the 16th century, was hexagonal. At its angles were pinacles and gargoyles. Six canopied niches contained figures of saints. At the top of the cross was a sun-dial, and the whole structure was surmounted by a weathercock which, probably under Puritan influence, superseded a cross or crucifix. The sketch in the British Museum displays the cross as surrounded by a roofed arcade, supported on six pillars. This arcade, which greatly detracts from the dignity and beauty of the cross, was almost certainly a later addition to the original. The cross was demolished in 1771 with the consent of the Bishop of Winchester. The present cross is a close reproduction of the main part of the former structure. It was presented to the town by Dr. Kinglake in 1867. Towards the South-West of the Market-place stood the Guildhall, built in the reign of Edward IV. This edifice in all probability was worthy of its name and an adornment to the town. Unfortunately for its reputation, its basement was made use of as two small narrow prisons. In these terrible cells, no fire could be made. There was no drainage. No water could be obtained except what was brought from outside by the Keeper. There was neither light nor air except the little that stole through a narrow grating in the door. A wooden platform, three feet above the floor, formed the "bedstead," on which the prisoners slept on straw.

Suitable nicknames had been found for these shocking cells. One of them was called "The Cow-

* See the lithograph of the Old Cross at the Public Library.

THE MARKET CROSS. REMOVED IN 1771.

house," the other, "Little Ease." Here deserters and vagrants expiated their offences. No punishment was more dreaded than confinement in one of these cells. Hardened criminals had been known to commit suicide rather than remain in such hideous surroundings.

Blocking most of the space necessary for the Market, and undoubtedly an encroachment upon it, were fourteen houses, crowding the area and forming a kind of plague spot in the centre of the business life of the town. Eleven of these houses were inns, and are described by the local historian, Savage, as "receptacles for idleness and vice."* The influence of these third-rate beer-houses was in every way demoralising. They encouraged drunkenness. They fostered that form of market bargaining over a glass in which the stronger head prevails at the expense of the weaker. Crowded and congested as these inns were, they were a potent means of disseminating disease.

It was a monstrous thing to have eleven inns of a small and disreputable type, spoiling the area of the Market, and competing with one another to lower the morals of those who frequented it.

The Market from the very commencement had been held along the streets and on such open spaces as were available. It can readily be imagined how inconvenient this arrangement must have been both to sellers and buyers, especially in bad weather. The exposure of

* These inns were named as follows: "The Salutation," "The Ball," "The Antelope," "The Bull," "The Lamb," "The Butchers' Arms," "The Rose and Crown," "The Wheatsheaf," "The Unicorn," and "The Sugar Loaf."

meat and other perishables under imperfect coverings to the heat and dust must have been fraught with injury to the consumers.

It was not, however, only the state of the Market which for years had outraged the feelings of the more enlightened citizens of the town. Decent inhabitants were shocked, and even kept within doors, by the state of things which prevailed in the streets at night. It was alleged with justice, "that many irregularities and disorders were frequently committed in the night time in East Street, High Street, North Street, and Fore Street."

The cause was stated to be the almost complete absence of effectual lighting. This "illumination" was probably confined to a few horn lanterns, separated by long distances, and emitting a glimmer which only made darkness visible. The feeble rays from these lanterns left the town the easy prey of the thieves, prostitutes and brawlers who infested the streets and robbed and insulted peaceable inhabitants. The scanty band of parish constables was powerless to deal with the evils which prevailed under cover of the darkness.

Such were the conditions under which our ancestors were still living little more than a century and a half ago, and at the time when Smollett visited the town. The evils were chronic and acute, and called for a remedy. Happily patriotic citizens were found determined at last to wrestle with them and bring about a change.

## CHAPTER V.

THE PLAN OF REFORM STARTED—A FORMER TAUNTON ELECTION—MARKET HOUSE SOCIETY—CANDIDATES FOR BOROUGH ALLOWED A WALK OVER AND SUBSCRIBE HEAVILY TO THE SOCIETY—ACT OF PARLIAMENT PASSED IN 1768 FORMING THE TRUST—DETAILS OF THE ACT—WIDE POWERS OF THE TRUST—MARKET SANITATION AND LIGHTING DEALT WITH—THE MARKET HOUSE—SAVAGE'S DESCRIPTION.

THE evils which so injured the health and credit of the town had lasted for years. The Mayor and Corporation had proved themselves incompetent to deal with them. Apparently they had neither the inclination nor the money to help in time of need. They adopted the easier course of doing nothing, and must have been the despair of the community. It was necessary to look elsewhere.

The question of a drastic alteration of existing conditions was openly discussed at a convivial meeting of some of the principal inhabitants of the town, in 1763. The guests realised that a liberal subscription would be necessary if anything worth doing were to be done. They reminded one another that bribes were lavished wholesale, and drunkenness and vice encouraged at every contested election. It was agreed that if the money thus wasted could be saved and utilised to improve the Market and the town, a work so long overdue could be immediately set in motion. Those present at the meeting must have remembered only too well the election of a single member caused by the death of Mr. Halliday, in 1754. It was then that the vacant seat was contested for six months. The memory of the shame and disgrace of that election doubtless stirred every guest to expressions of horror and indignation. During the whole of the six months immediately preceding the election, the candidates debauched their supporters at the inns in the town, where drinks were to be had at any time for nothing. Many of the electors fell into utter idleness and dissipation. The town reeked with drink and noise. Street fighting was an every day incident. Many townsmen were maimed and wounded; several lost their lives. The member returned was carried from the poll to his lodgings followed by disappointed opponents, frantic with rage and drink, and thirsting for his life. He was considered fortunate in escaping from their clutches without losing life or limb in the battle which raged round his person.

During that tempestuous six months, very little work was done in Taunton. The woollen manufactory seriously declined, as orders sent for execution could not be dealt with and were returned. The fair fame and prosperity of the town were seriously set back by this election. It was no wonder that decent people asked themselves the question, "To what purpose is this waste?" Those who were bent on the improvement of the Market were equally anxious to prevent such another disgrace as the election of 1754.

The men responsible for formulating the plan of diverting the money spent by candidates on corrupting the constituency to the useful end of benefiting the town soon found many converts. An Association, called

" The Market-house Society," was formed. The scheme of the promoters was to bring about an uncontested election at the earliest possible date. The candidates were to pledge themselves to devote the amount usually spent on " bribery and feasting " to this act of " public and permanent utility." In other words, the sum thus obtained was to be employed in the work of regenerating the town by giving it a suitable market, a market-house, and properly lighting the streets. It was not for five years that the scheme, first evolved at the " convivial meeting " and then taken over by the Market-house Society, bore fruit. The influence of Benjamin Hammet, afterwards one of the borough members, helped greatly to bring about the desired result. Two candidates who had already begun to canvas the constituency in the usual corrupt style were induced to withdraw. The election of the two other candidates, A. Popham and Nathaniel Webb, was in consequence a walk over. These new members took their seats, and Webb paid the bill. Unscrupulous voters lost their guineas and their beer, but the town was rescued from disrepute. Two thousand pounds were paid to forward the purposes of the Market-house Society. The clear inference is that this was the large sum which candidates had to spend when wooing the suffrages of five or six hundred electors.* The new members came out of the transaction most honourably. Not only was the money paid, but they devoted their energies to obtaining an Act of

* The total of further subscriptions given by country gentlemen of the neighbourhood and leading inhabitants of the town ultimately reached about three thousand pounds.

Parliament which should carry out the ends of the Market-house Society. This Act was passed in the very year of their election.

An examination of the Act will show with what thoroughness and care the details were worked out by those who framed it. The Act which constituted the Market Trust did in fact nothing less than make the Market Trustees the supreme authority in the town. Gone was the power of the Court Leet. The second Corporation indeed remained till its ignominious end, but with clipped wings, and possessing only judicial and electoral powers, and the control of the town charities. Few members of such a Corporation could have died of overwork, and there is no record of any such catastrophe. The markets, the sanitation, and the lighting of the town were vested in Trustees. The borrowing of the sum of £4,000 was sanctioned for the purpose of carrying out the objects of the Trust. The interest of this sum was charged on the rents and profits of the Market.

Small annuities were to be paid to the Bishop of Winchester and the Portreeves for the loss of such Market rights as they still possessed. Any balance in the hands of the Trustees was to be applied to the clothing, educating, and placing out apprentices in St. Mary's Parish. Though the apprentices' bell is still rung at St. Mary's Church, it rouses no somnolent apprentices. That system has passed away. When the Trust is finally discharged, it can benefit no apprentices. It was ordered that two-thirds of the Trustees should be inhabitants of the town. One-third were to be residents in the adjacent villages. The interests of the town and of country-people supplying and frequenting the Market were thus respected. The disreputable inns and houses were to be demolished, to furnish a site for the Market. Regret must be felt that the ancient Guildhall, which had weathered the storms of three centuries, was condemned. Let us hope that its destruction was a painful necessity. The present Parade was thus to be cleared of buildings and a market held upon it as before. The old Assembly Rooms of which we know little or nothing, except that they were the property of a private individual, were also to be removed. Two disreputable old houses between "Groping Lane" and "Horse Lane," which obstructed the approach to North Town Bridge, were to be cleared away. The very name of the former of these lanes is suggestive of the difficulties which beset pedestrians in threading their way through this labyrinth in the darkness. The streets and passages of the town were "to be cleansed, and freed from all annoyances, obstructions, nuisances, and encroachments whatever." The ramblings of swine through the streets, already familiar to us, were not forgotten, and were to be checked. The Trustees were to control the sale, not only of live cattle, but of corn, meat, fish, poultry, fruit, and other perishables. Nothing of this description was to be exposed for sale either in the streets or anywhere else within a thousand yards of the Market. Corn dealers, butchers, poulterers, and fishmongers were thus tied to the Market, and had to pay for the necessary licenses. Goldsworthy could remember how, in the earlier years of the last century, "the butchers' shambles stood in rows on the Parade from south to north." He tells us, moreover, that "the Fish

Market was close under the Guildhall windows." The sitting magistrates must have realised that fish is less esteemed for its perfume than its taste. "Glass lamps," a novelty which almost dumbfounded our ancestors with wonder and admiration, were to supersede the dingy old horn lanterns, and to be placed in East Street, High Street, North Street, and Fore Street. Such were the directions of the Act of Parliament to the Market Trust, and all were faithfully carried out by the Trustees.

The same body also in 1770 erected the present Market House on the site of the old Assembly Room, and the adjoining Arcades.

The work was added to in 1772. Of this Market House, which is of a chaste and simple appearance, "simplex munditiis," Tauntonians were justly proud. They would probably have started back in amazement, had they realised that the idea of its demolition would ever be seriously spoken of. Our historian, Savage, grows eloquent when he describes the Market House, with which he was almost as impressed as the Queen of Sheba with the glories of Solomon. He describes it as "an elegant building." "The house," he says, "which is in the centre, is laid out into different apartments for the purposes of Justice, amusement and pleasure." After speaking of its lesser glories, the Guildhall, the reading-room, the card-room, the billiard-room, he passes to "the superb assembly-room, fifty feet long, thirty feet wide, and twenty-four feet high, with a music-gallery." "This room," he adds, "is furnished with two elegant and large glass chandeliers." With a mention of "the portrait of George III., placed opposite the music gallery, painted while he was Prince of Wales," Savage closes his description of the Market House.

All those who reverence the past, all who recognise how useful this Market House has been for a hundred and fifty years, all who see in it a building dear to our ancestors, and trodden by six generations of men and women bent on politics, business or amusement, will never sanction its destruction or mutilation. Gone are the days when protests against such outrages as the casting to the ground of the old towers of St. Mary's and St. James' were made in vain. The Market House is consecrated by many memories, and will live to be hallowed by many more.

## CHAPTER VI.

FALL OF SECOND CORPORATION—MARKET TRUSTEES THE SOLE AUTHORITY—FRUITLESS PETITIONS FOR A NEW CHARTER—HAMMET'S ACTIVITIES—PAVING—THE CASTLE —HAMMET STREET AND ST. MARY'S CHURCH—INCREASE OF MARKET TOLLS—A FRESH ACT OF PARLIAMENT—MEAT MARKET—CATTLE MARKET—INTRODUCTION OF GAS.

WE have to picture the town as, for many years from 1768, under the control of the new authority, the Market Trustees. The Corporation, granted by Charles II., did indeed continue its lethargic procedure until 1792. At that date, it terminated its inglorious existence. It really committed suicide. It had failed to keep up its numbers to the required level. Indeed the figure had dropped from twenty-five to eleven. Thus the Corporation contained not even half the requisite number of members. There is nothing to show that there were lamentation and great mourning when this indolent body passed into the domain of history. The town could console itself. It had its energetic Market Trustees, men who always proved themselves efficient and had done, and were doing, so much to fulfil the purposes of the Trust. There were certainly some, twenty years afterwards, who hankered after the flesh pots of Egypt, and made two attempts to win back the forfeited charter. When these efforts were made first in 1810, and then again in 1814, no attack was launched against the management of the town by the Market Trustees. No one ventured to say that the Market was not greatly improved. No denial was made of the fact that the lighting, paving and scavenging were infinitely better than in "the good old days" of the last Corporation. The petitioners contented themselves with urging that law and justice were now in the hands of the county magistrates, and that the supply of constables was insufficient. How much better it would be if the terrors of the law belonged to a resident bench of magistrates, and this consummation would be the direct result of a fresh charter! The petition came at length before the Privy Council. The arguments of the petitioners were considered by the Council. Their prayer was rejected. More residents in Taunton, however, were put on the county bench. The main grievance was thus redressed, but the Market Trustees remained masters of the situation.

While the town was under the sway of the Trustees, who were at all events doing something to cleanse the Augean stables which it had become, it owed a great debt also to the activities of one of its borough members, Sir Benjamin Hammet. This patriotic citizen, as will be remembered, had exerted himself to procure the agreement about the election of 1768, which enabled the Market House Society to begin its work. Since those days, Hammet had been knighted and the borough had honoured itself and him by giving him the highest distinction in its power. Hammet began life as a porter in a London bookseller's shop, rose to be an eminent banker in Lombard Street, became an Alderman of the City, and was knighted by George III. He had a large house at Sherford, near Taunton, part of the garden wall of which may still be seen, and also possessed a seat in Wales, where he died in 1800.

Living constantly at Sherford, he was able to maintain the closest touch with his constituents. Hammet had devoted every effort to the paving of the principal streets. He also did what he could to restore the Castle, which had been in ruins since it was dismantled after the Restoration. It is probably true to say that, like most of his contemporaries, he did not possess sufficient antiquarian or architectural knowledge for such an undertaking. In 1788, he began the great task which should endear his memory to all Tauntonians. He procured an Act of Parliament to deal with the approach to St. Mary's Church, and quickly proceeded to carry his design into execution. St. Mary's Church had been one of the glories of the town long before it struck the attention of Henry VII. on his visit to the Priory during Warbeck's rebellion. If tradition may be trusted, the King showed his appreciation by the present of a new tower and middle aisle. His head, graven by a cunning hand, and adorning the chancel arch of the Church, is a perpetual witness of his interest and of a generosity which forms a striking contrast to his usual parsimony. Through all the vicissitudes of its history, those born under the shadow of St. Mary's have always regarded it with affection. Nonconformists have venerated the Church, not less so because they have remembered that the first pastor of Paul's Meeting had for many years been its Vicar. The Church, however, had become like a fair jewel in a poor setting. At the close of the 18th century, it was encompassed on all sides by alleys containing houses of the worst description, the homes of the

HAMMET STREET AND ST. MARY'S TOWER.

bullies, thieves, drunkards, and prostitutes who disgraced the town. Some of these houses lingered on for more than another hundred years. They are remembered with disgust by very old persons still living.

There was, moreover, no tolerable approach to the Church. The site now occupied by Hammet Street was a festering mass of squalid houses. The only means of access lay through a narrow lane containing a ruinous almshouse and opening between the shops now occupied by Messrs. Midelton and Boots. This lane led out into an alley about half-way down the present Hammet Street, and through this the Church was reached. It was with extreme difficulty, and not without endangering the lives of pedestrians, that a carriage could convey its occupants to the Sunday services. Hammet obtained power under the Act, not only to sweep away the dens that blocked the way to the sanctuary, but also to demolish several houses in Fore Street, tenanted by substantial citizens. He than laid out Hammet Street in a direct line to St. Mary's, and built the existing houses at his own expense. Hammet took care that the new street, called after his name, should end in a wide open space, known as Church Square.

Savage tells us that the new street proved most attractive. According to him, it was particularly in favour with "the genteel and well informed society which inhabited the town."

In 1807, the building of the houses, known as "The Crescent," was commenced. Those who reside in them will be pleased to hear that our historian describes them "as a range of elegant houses, calculated for the residence of genteel families."

These improvements in the town are closely connected with the work of the Market Trustees. They had been the pioneers of reform. The changes made by them had made others worth doing. Taunton had become a better place to live in, and good houses were more likely to find tenants than formerly.

The quality of the new Market was proved by the rapidly increasing tolls. These payments, which in those days were farmed, were let, in 1792, for £460 yearly, and in 1799 for £510. In 1813 the sum had increased to £942; by 1820 to £1,370; and by 1826 to £1,500.

The advance in the prosperity of the town was so great, and its Market so frequented, that still more accommodation for the latter became needful. A second Act of Parliament was therefore obtained in 1817, with the view of securing the necessary improvements. The Trustees were permitted to borrow ten thousand pounds to carry them out. The result soon appeared. Houses were bought and pulled down, and the buildings now known as the Meat Market and New Market House erected. The butchers had no longer to expose their meat on the Parade. They were now housed in an airy and comfortable building, and the meat secured from injury by dust and heat. For over a century this meat market has attracted all the best butchers to the town, with the result of improving the standard of the meat and keeping the price at a fair level.

Space was also left for other stalls, and vendors of fruit, vegetables, books, and other commodities have always been in occupation. In those days too glovers, hatters, ropers, bakers, and confectioners took stalls in the Market. The Parade became available on Saturdays for these, as also for itinerant dealers. Any policy of closing the Parade to dealers would not only destroy a picturesque and old world scene on Saturdays, but would be an interference with a legitimate competition.

The Trustees were permitted by the new Act to light not merely the main arteries of the town, but also the side streets. The old horn lanterns which had shed anything but a kindly light amidst the encircling gloom, had been superseded, as we have seen, by " glass lamps " burning oil. These oil lamps, forty years before, had been the admiration of those who profited by them. An incandescent gas, then a recent scientific discovery, was to take the place of oil, which has, in its turn, been since superseded by the electric light.

It is clear that the town had made enormous strides forward since 1768, the year when the Market Trust was born.

Yet though Taunton, in 1820, was a very much cleaner and more habitable place than in 1768, we should hardly tolerate the condition of things which even then prevailed. Silver Street, we are assured, was " a dirty and very immoral place." The same writer, who spoke from personal recollections, tells us that " all the houses in East Reach were thatched and fires frequent."

"Bath Place was a rough and dirty court. At the bottom of it, close to the archway, was an open drain, wherein all the abominations from the courts in High Street and the Crescent houses were seen passing down.

North Street was low, dirty and damp at all seasons of the year. It had a nasty open black-and-green seething ditch."

These are but illustrations to show that, even after the great work of the Market Trustees, and Hammet's efforts, there remained many an evil that cried aloud for remedy. Much had been done, much more remained to do. As we look back over a hundred years, and contrast the past with the present, we shall find it difficult to discover anything in which our ancestors excelled ourselves. It would, on the other hand, be easy to show that in every outward circumstance, in all that tends to the health, comfort, and even the moral well being of the community, our situation is infinitely better than theirs.

## CHAPTER VII.

THE FIRST MINUTE BOOK—MR. WAKE'S EXTRACTS—EMINENT TRUSTEES—ORIGINAL NUMBER—A QUORUM—NOTICES AND PLACES OF MEETINGS—TOLLS FIXED—MOUNTEBANK STAGES—PUMPS—SIGN-BOARDS—BARBERS' POLLS—WHEELBARROWS—NAUGHTY BOYS—MAY 29TH—MARKET HOURS—COMPENSATION FOR INJURIES—FRICTION WITH CORPORATION—"MR. CORNELIUS"—SCAVENGERS—A SQUIRE-SCAVENGER AND A PARSON-SCAVENGER—LIGHTING.

THE first Minute Book of the Market Trustees was among those consulted by Mr. W. H. Wake, the present Clerk to the Trustees, in preparing a lecture entitled, "A Survey of the Market Trust." This paper was read before the Taunton Chamber of Commerce in 1908. Mr. Wake, on that occasion, read many extracts from the first Minute Book, chosen by him with great care and discrimination. The present account of the curiosities of this Minute Book is based on his extracts, and on an examination kindly granted by him of the book itself. It begins with an account of the first meeting of the Trust, on January 4th, 1769. It concludes with a meeting held on March 28th, 1800. This ancient folio, redolent of the past, which has been thumbed and worn by many of our ancestors, is most illuminating, and will be invaluable to the future historian of Taunton. It contains the signatures of Benjamin Hammet, Copplestone, Warre-Bamfflyde, Joshua Toulmin, the historian, the two Pophams, and many other benefactors of the town, "now gone down to Hades, even many gallant souls of heroes."

There is a list of the ninety-eight original Trustees. Each subscriber of five guineas or upwards to the purposes of the Trust became one of these Trustees. Vacancies were filled by co-option after the number had fallen below sixty. Among the first Trustees were many who bore names quite familiar to ourselves. Those of Acland, Tynte, Lethbridge, Warre, Sanford, Anderdon, Popham, Welman, Hammet are indeed well known to all Somerset people. It will be remembered that two thousand pounds of the original sum of £2,877 16s. 0d., subscribed for the purposes of the Trust, and afterwards increased to over five thousand pounds, were given by one of the members who took their seats for the borough without a contest in 1768. There were at first, as a rule, about thirty meetings of the Trustees every year. Nine members formed a quorum, and owing to insufficient numbers present, the meetings were often adjourned. They were advertised by a *viva voce* notice in St. Mary's Church, on the Sunday previous to each meeting. For his expenditure of voice power, Spiller, the Parish Clerk, received the sum of sixpence for each notice. The effort did not kill him, for he lived to give the notice perhaps a thousand times. The Vicar of the Parish must have felt inclined to follow up the notice with sermons either on the "children sitting in the market-place," or on those "standing idle in the market-place."

The original meeting-place of the Trustees was the old Guildhall. When that was pulled down, the Trustees went to the old Assembly Rooms. When this room shared the fate of the Guildhall, the meetings were held at the White Hart Inn. After the erection of the Market House, they took place at what is always called "The Town Hall," which is in fact the present Guildhall.

The buying out the old occupiers of the Parade site, the destruction of their houses, the Guildhall, the old Assembly Rooms and the Market Cross were among the earlier works of the Trust. The fixing of the tolls was another important matter. When the tolls were settled, they were let to contractors at a fixed sum for a term of years, and the Trustees were thus free from the trouble of collecting. Prosecutions on their part, however, were threatened, or took place, when the tolls were evaded. The Trustees, at an early date, had to deal with "mountebank stages," on which doubtless acrobats performed, which they found at the doors of "the Half Moon" and "the Three Cups." These they ordered to be removed. They also swept off from the streets Miss Jane Baily, who had "a right in the broom-market, held at Mr. Francis Capon's door." Miss Baily, however, swept in five pounds as compensation from the Trustees. Brooms were afterwards sold in the Market itself. These brooms were bought from the "broom-squires," who also sold poached hares and pheasants in a quiet way and on reasonable terms. They were in consequence unpopular with other squires.

The Trustees noticed that the pumps in the town were often in front of the houses in the streets. Passers-by complained that they were frequently deluged with water from these pumps. The Trustees commanded that the spouts should be placed in a less imperilling position.

Protruding sign-boards were in those days suspended

over nearly every shop, as well as over the inns. There was little else to mark the shops, for the panes of glass in them were small, and the practice of window-dressing hardly started till the middle of the last century.

Readers of "Macaulay's History" will be reminded of his description of the shops in London, in 1685, as "distinguished by painted or sculptured signs, which gave a gay and grotesque aspect to the streets.

"The walk from Charing Cross to Whitechapel lay through an endless succession of Saracens' Heads, Royal Oaks, Blue Bears, and Golden Lambs, which disappeared when they were no longer required for the direction of the common people." The Taunton Trustees must have thought but little of "the gay and grotesque," when they ordered these signs to be removed and insulted them by calling them "nuisances."

Nearly thirty years later, they attacked the fraternity of the barbers who, for many years, had joked on the word "poll," by placing "a barber's pole" outside their shops. These polls, said the Trustees, must either be removed, or placed upright against the houses.

The question of obstructions arose from time to time. Shop-keepers who ventured to have windows or balconies encroaching into the streets beyond their old limits, were sternly told to remove them. Carriages were not allowed to remain long stationary and block the streets. Though perambulators did not then exist, and so could not be driven three abreast, wheelbarrows were a trouble to pedestrians. An order was accordingly made, in 1799, "that five boards be made and fixed up to prevent people from driving wheelbarrows on the pavement." Years before, the whole subject of nuisances and obstructions had been dealt with by the circulation of five hundred copies of the Act dealing with them. An addition was made that anyone incapable of paying the fine should be committed to the House of Correction.

Carpet-beating in the streets is an interesting spectacle which has not often been seen by anyone now living. It was evidently by no means uncommon in those days, but the Trustees would have none of it. The maxim that " boys will be boys " was checked by the Argus-eyed Trustees.

Were boys, they said, to shout and hoot in the Arcades? Were they actually to be permitted to spin tops or play marbles in the same sacred precincts or on the Parade? Were they to throw stones with impunity and thus perhaps hit the person of a Market Trustee?

Against any easy tolerance the Trustees set their faces, and measures were taken to confine the sportiveness of the rising generation within reasonable limits.

Old inhabitants of the town will remember the time when the Restoration of Charles II. was celebrated on his birthday, May 29th, by the setting up of oak boughs outside the inns of the town. The former Trustees had every reason to malign the day when the Merry Monarch spent by no means a festive time, hidden amidst the thick branches of an oak, and stealthily watched the soldiers of Cromwell, who were looking for him everywhere except in the tree. Not merely was it customary with Tauntonians to place great boughs of oak at their doors on May 29th, but they even broke up the pavements to do so. The Trustees thought that this was carrying loyalty to the memory of " His Sacred Majesty " a little too far, and did their utmost to stop the injury to the pavements. "The Bellman," said the Trustees, "is to give notice to the inhabitants that it will not be permitted, and if anyone attempts to break up the said pavements, they will be prosecuted as the law directs." By an order passed in 1770, the "Fowl Market" was fixed to begin at 8 a.m. and end at noon, and the Corn Market to begin at noon and end at 3 p.m. The butchers, bakers, cheesemongers, and other trades were to begin their business at 8 a.m., and to end it at 7 p.m. In 1795, the hour of closing was altered to 8 p.m. The market bell was to indicate the various hours of the opening and closing of the Markets. The bell was rung in the first instance by "Mr. Cornelius," of whom we shall hear more presently.

The Parade was bounded and fenced in by oak posts gilded at the top, with chains between them. Iron posts were afterwards substituted, but there are many who must remember the old chains. They should have been left. They really were "links" with the past.

The Trustees did not err on the side of lavishness when, as we are told, two of their workmen had "each an arm broke" by the fall of a chimney, when "the Antelope," one of the beer-houses on the Island, was pulled down. They paid the surgeon who attended the men, and allowed the latter six shillings a week each as long as incapacitated. This sum is perhaps equivalent to a pound of our present currency. There was some little friction between the new Trustees and the old Corporation. The latter had the right of using the new Guildhall for the borough bench of magistrates. They locked the door between the Guildhall and the "back parlour," and ordered their servant, "Mr. Cornelius," not to give the Trustees a key. The Trustees retaliated by entering the room from outside, bolting the locked door and thus cutting off the Corporation from its use. "Mr. Cornelius," who was, as we have seen, also in the employ of the Trustees as bell-ringer, lost that appointment owing to this dispute. Soon afterwards he had to give up his house on "the Island," and an order was made "that the cellars of 'Mr. Cornelius' be filled with rubbish."

It was not, we may be sure, without excellent reason, that the question of the proper scavenging of the town engaged the constant attention of the Trustees. The "scavengers" for many years had to get the work done from love for the community and were paid nothing. The first scavengers under the Market Trust were three of the Trustees themselves, but they only undertook the work for a fortnight. At the next meeting, "John Mallack, Esq., is appointed scavenger for the streets and lanes of St. Mary's." Mallack, who was the Lord of the Manor, was to pay the Trustees five pounds a year for the honour. His coadjutor, the scavenger for St. James' Parish, was James Minifie, a clergyman. Possibly out of regard for his cloth, he paid nothing for the privilege, except the sums expended on his deputies. Both these gentlemen were Trustees. We find similar records for some time afterwards. "The scavengership," as the Minute Book in one place terms it, was held, in 1780, by Mr. James Hare, one of the Trustees. His district consisted of Fore Street, High Street, East Street, and North Street. Hare was to have the work done at his own expense, and to give security for twenty pounds.

The offer of a salary in 1791 seems to have brought no candidate; for, a month afterwards, we find a Committee appointed to superintend the scavenging of the various streets.

In 1795, Mr. James Haviland was appointed scavenger at a salary of £10 per annum. He eventually died a bankrupt.

In 1796, three gentlemen were promoted to be scavengers for a year. The Minute says of them: "They engages to sweep the streets twice every week and to carry off the slush immediately." As a slush cart had been provided by the Trustees some years before, and was perhaps not yet worn out, the task of the scavengers was facilitated. Moreover, an allowance seems by this time to have been made for "sweepers," and we hear of a guinea a year for broom money.

Scavenging then evidently presented a great deal of difficulty in those days, and, when all was done, a perfume which we should not like probably lingered in the Streets.

Lighting the town was also a matter constantly before the minds of the Trustees, and they seem to have done their utmost in the matter. The number of lamps for High Street, Fore Street, North Street, and East Street was originally fixed at forty, but this figure was increased more than once.

The payment for lighting was originally fifteen shillings and sixpence yearly for each lamp. The sum rose to a pound, fell to seventeen shillings, and rose again to nineteen shillings. "The said lamps," says a Minute, "are to be lighted each night before it is dark and continue to burn until two in the morning, except seven days before and one day after the full moon."

THE PARADE, MARKET HOUSE AND ARCADES IN THE COACHING DAYS.

## CHAPTER VIII.

MORE DETAILS—THE BEADLE—THE "NEW MARKET PLACE"—THE CATTLE MARKET—BUTCHERS' LICENSES—SCAVENGING GOES FORWARD—RHINE RIDDERS—WATERING AND WATER CARTS—DRAINAGE—MORE LIGHT—THE TOLLS—WOMBWELL'S VISIT—"UP IN A BALLOON"—HUSTINGS—COFFEE STALLS—GLASSES AND BROKEN GLASS—"REGRATING AND FORESTALLING."

FURTHER particulars gleaned from the earlier Minute Books may be interesting. The Market Trustees found it necessary from the first to engage the services of a clerk. They have always been most faithfully served. As time went on, other officers were appointed. In 1817, for example, a beadle was advertised for, to deal with "nuisances and penalties." His duties were more clearly defined, in 1826, as "superintendence of the cleaning of the streets and Market-place, issuing summonses, and removing disorderly men and women from the streets." On more than one occasion, the beadle was directed to prosecute people "who exercised horses in the streets," and converted them into a kind of Rotten Row. The first beadle was William Batt. His salary was fixed at £15, and soon raised to £20. He was to be resplendent in a great-coat and cocked hat, which were to last three years. He also bore a staff of office. Unless his apparel had seen the three years out, he was to hand it, as well as his staff, to his successor. The cocked hat cost £3 3s. 0d.; the clothes £12 9s. 0d. Even beadles are mortal, and some are not infallible. When Batt's "fell arrest" came, his successor seems to have proved himself an unprofitable beadle. After a reign of only two years, he was discharged. He had to surrender "his last coat, waistcoat and cocked hat," but was allowed to retain "his old clothes and glazed hat." The beadle was already the "crier or bellman," and in 1838 we find him "the Clerk of the Market." He must have been ready to sink under such a weight of dignity.

Few records remain of people so reprobate as to defy a beadle. In 1846, however, when "a show of wild beasts" had been placed on the Parade, apparently without authority, an attempt was made by representatives of the Trustees to remove it. This effort was resisted, and the beadle defied. "How were the mighty fallen"! Eventually a beadle failed to carry out the instructions of the clerk. He was dismissed and the office ceased to exist.

It has been mentioned that, early in the last century, the Trustees built what are now known as the Victoria Rooms, with the Market area beneath. This building was originally called "the new Market-place." Here for five days in succession was celebrated the Coronation Festival of the Queen in 1838. The name Victoria was not, however, given to "the new Market House" until 1876. The large room was originally a "Free Exchange Room" on Saturdays. There dealers could show samples and make bargains. On other days, it might be used for auctions, sales and exhibitions. In a few years, it was let to a Reading Institution. There must be many who remember when the "Reading Institution" occupied one-half of the room and the Museum the other.

Archæologists were gratified by being able to find antiquities equally curious in the Reading Room and the Museum.

Corn, fish, poultry, butter, and cheese were sold in the New Market-place. The Cattle Market was for some time fixed to be held in "East Reach, between the space opposite Tancred Street and the Spittle Turnpike Gate." It was afterwards moved to the north side of East Reach, then to a field in East Reach, then again to "Pugsley's field," and finally, in 1841, to Castle Green. It was thus for some time a kind of travelling show. Cattle could only be sold in the town in accordance with the decrees of the Trustees. When, in 1840, "oxen and sheep were offered for sale at Mr. Barrett's Bazaar," the Trustees protested. Mr. Barrett was told that he was flying in the face of an Act of Parliament. He may well have trembled when informed that a prosecution would follow if his offence were repeated.

The larger part of the income of the Trustees was derived from the licences taken out by the butchers who, for three-quarters of a century, were only allowed to sell in the Market itself.

Within the memory of many still living, this right was once more insisted on, and every butcher's shop within 1,000 yards of the Parade was closed. The only butcher's shop then open lay just outside the radius, near Abbot Bere's old leper-house. In June, 1828, "Mr. Miles made application, on the part of Mr. Drake, to open a shop for selling pork in the town." The petition was rejected. In September, 1828, Mr. W. P. Pinchard reported "that Charles Davey had been convicted in the penalty of five pounds for sale of meat contrary to Act of Parliament." In 1835, however, a license was granted for the sale of meat, except on Sundays, to Mr. Warren, at the shop in East Street, now occupied by Mr. Medway. In 1840, it was decided that three more butcher's shops should be licensed on condition that each of these butchers should take two stalls in the Market on Saturdays, and one on other days, and pay an additional fifteen pounds per annum. The offer did not at first prove attractive, for it was not until 1842 that even one more butcher's shop was started. This new shop was established near the old North Town Bridge by Thomas Newton.*

Only so recently as 1834 were fixed butchers' stalls set up in the Market. Until then, they had been moveable. It was now that "thirteen butchers' stalls with heads" were constructed and twenty butchers' stalls of a lighter type set up in the centre of the Pork Market.

In connection with the improvement of the Butchers' Market, a small parcel of land was bought from the Trustees of the Grammar School. We read with regret that "the entrance archway from the Castle Gateway" to the Grammar School was removed. What was this but the butchery of a fragment of a seat of learning?

The scavenging of the town was now let sometimes to one, sometimes to several individuals. We read that, in 1825, "the cleansing of the streets from the Full Moon to the Western Turnpike Gate be granted to William Spiller, he engaging to do it for nothing." The other streets were let to two contractors for forty-two

* Newton's shop was next to the Horse Pond, and is now occupied by a greengrocer.

pounds. The scavenging was sometimes supervised by Committees, and, in 1829, it was ordered that "no salary shall be paid without a certificate signed by the Beadle that the scavengers have done their duty." This regulation was frequently carried into effect. Samuel Allen for some years enjoyed the privilege of "the sweeping, cleaning and weeding of Hammet Street, Church Square, Whirligig Lane, Blackboy Lane, and Magdalene Lane, for which he was paid 1 9 weekly." The "filth," however, was removed by the superior scavengers. Allen liked his work, or his pay, well enough to continue his duties for a long period. Fidelity and ambition are sometimes rewarded, and Allen at last was drawing three shillings weekly.

A payment of two guineas per annum was made to "the rhine-ridders" of the Court Leet, until the rhines running along the streets were swept away in the middle of the last century.

The year 1822 provides the first mention of a water-cart and, three years later, two men were appointed to "water the streets as often as the Beadle thinks proper at three shillings a time." For some time water-carts were discontinued, and a "hand-engine" substituted; but in 1842 we find the Trustees in possession of two water-carts. There were formerly "tithing pumps" in each of the "tithings" into which Taunton was once divided, and there are those living who can remember the tithing-pump in Paul Street. The Trustees, however, found that the tithing-pumps, which were probably unduly taxed before, could not yield a sufficient supply of water for the carts. They spent at least two hundred pounds in boring for water in Mount Street, apparently without result. At last Mr. Jeboult reported that "a pump for supplying water had been erected on the town bridge and found to answer the purpose." The Trustees began to consider the question of what the Minute Book describes as "subterenous sewers," in 1817. When action followed discussion, only the principal streets were at first dealt with, and inhabitants were expected to contribute for collateral drains. It was many years before the side streets had any drainage at all. The drainage of towns was a new experiment in England, though it existed in the ancient world among the Romans and, as recent excavations have shown, in Crete, long before their day. The Trustees found constant difficulties as the drainage proceeded. It was complained, for example, that the navigation of the river was impeded by the sewage which was discharged into it.

Dr. Alford has alluded to the frequency of open sewers in those days. One of them lay at the back of North Street. River, streams and wells were all polluted and, in consequence, typhoid fever claimed many victims. Much of the drainage at last passed into the hands of a Company which depended for its profits on its charge for making collateral drains.

The number of lamps in the town had greatly increased by 1840, when their number was 120. The price of lighting, which, in 1800, had been less than a pound for each lamp, stood in the middle of the century at the sum of fifteen shillings. The system of lighting which prevailed until about 1880 involved the carrying of a short ladder by each lamp-lighter. With this he proceeded quickly from lamp to lamp, and with mounting the ladder and lighting each lamp, had plenty to do for his money. The Trustees worked in conjunction with the Gas Company. The value of the tolls continued to rise, and the expenses of the Trustees nearly equalled them. The tolls were let, in 1826, for £1,500; in 1833, for £1,600. There were no borough rates, so all the expenses of the Trustees, including the interest of their debt, were met from the profits of the licenses and letting the rooms which they owned. It is extraordinary that they could do what they did without any direct call on the resources of the community.

The Trustees sometimes allowed the presence of a Menagerie on the Parade. Wombwell, in 1843, applied for this permission, and agreed to make good any damage. Menageries were still sometimes found on the Parade in the sixties. How the tradesmen in Fore Street, who then usually lived at their business houses, could tolerate the roaring of the lions and other sonorous menagerie melodies cannot be easily explained. The Parade has often been used for displays of fireworks.

Aviation was in its infancy in the middle of the last century, and the only means of ascent in the air was the balloon. Great, doubtless, was the excitement in the town when "Green, the aeronaut," ascended from the Cattle Market, in August, 1846. He had previously agreed with the Trustees to pay for any walls that might be taken down and to make good all damage. Agricultural shows were often held in the Cattle Market, and, in 1856, and for a short time afterwards, when not used for the markets, it served as a playground for the old Grammar School of the town.

When candidates for Parliament, whether for the western part of the county or for the town, were nominated, the ceremony took place on a temporary platform erected on the Parade, called the hustings. On each side of this structure stood the opposing candidates and their nominators. The ceremony was accompanied by adulatory speeches of the nominators and professions of uncommon gratitude by the candidates. It was decided by the Trustees, on February 6th, 1835, "That Joseph Manning do receive three pounds for packing and erecting hustings on the market-place on the day of nomination of candidates for West Somerset."

The Whig candidates were returned by an enormous majority over their Conservative opponents.

Some who lived in the days when Plancus was consul have mentioned that, when starting in the early morning, on some fair spring day of the forties, they refreshed themselves with a nice cup of coffee under the Arcades. The licensed victuallers of the town, who seem to have had little love of coffee, presented on one occasion a petition to the Trustees against the presence of these stalls.

The Trustees decided that coffee should not be sold on the stalls before 5 a.m., and that "the stall-holders should be cleared off at 9.30 a.m." An extension of the latter hour was granted on market days.

Henry Labouchere, afterwards known as Lord Taunton, who became a Cabinet Minister, as President of the Board of Trade, represented Taunton in the Whig interest from 1830 to 1857. He was opposed, in 1835, by Disraeli, who described himself, in the course of the election, as "an Israelite in whom was no guile." Labouchere was triumphantly returned. If Disraeli had no guile in those days, he certainly had a large supply afterwards. Let us hope that he did not acquire it at Taunton.

In 1830, Labouchere intimated to the Trustees that he wished to present the town with "a public clock." The offer was gratefully accepted. It was at first proposed to place this clock in the parapet of the "new Market House." Eventually, however, it was set in its present position, where it has counted out "the sly slow hours" to four generations of "word-speaking men." The clock was formerly frequently termed "the Labouchere."

Mention has already been made incidentally of festivities in the town on the occasion of Queen Victoria's coronation. When William IV. was crowned, seven years before, many glasses were drunk and much glass belonging to the Trustees was broken. The Trustees made due allowances and repaired the damage, without asking any questions.

Students of mediæval history will remember in what horror the practices of "regrating" and "forestalling" were held by our ancestors. "Regrating" was buying corn or other provisions and selling them at an enhanced price in the same market. "Forestalling" was buying these goods before they actually arrived at the market, with the intention of raising their price in that market.

These practices were brought to the notice of the Trustees in 1837. The Clerk was directed to warn offenders against them. He was also told "to prosecute if necessary."

## CHAPTER IX.

POSITION OF TRUSTEES IN 1846—LOCAL BOARDS OF HEALTH—TAUNTON IMPROVEMENT AND MARKET BILL QUASHED—NUISANCE COMMITTEE—A SECOND BILL—ITS FATE—BOARD OF HEALTH ESTABLISHED—A HAPPY UNION—DIFFICULTIES ABOUT LIGHTING—CLEANSING AND WATERING SETTLED—UPHILL WORK WITH UPHILL DRAINS—QUIS CUSTODIET?—LICENSES—THE FISH HAWKER AND THE SALMON.

THE powers of the Trustees, especially in matters relating to the health of the town, were increased by Acts of Parliament, passed in the third year of William IV.'s reign, and the third of Victoria's.

These Acts, moreover, gave further borrowing powers. The annual income of the Trust continued to increase. It stood, in 1846, at over two thousand, one hundred and eighty pounds per annum. Expenses, however, continued to rise. The situation of the Trustees in the middle of the last century was not an easy one. They were expected to run the markets, lighting and debt of the town on quite a small income. They could impose no rates. They paid off some of their bonds when they could. Their powers of borrowing were restricted, and, moreover, they believed that debt increases the ultimate difficulty, even though at times it is inevitable. That principle is forgotten in these days of soaring debts and soaring rates.

The Trustees, however, with the best intentions in the world, had been gradually reaching an impossible

THE PARADE, WITH MARKET STALLS, ABOUT 1845.

position. The growing demand for really good drainage, sanitation and lighting, which was loudly expressed throughout the country, rendered action of some kind necessary. Sanitation was in the political and social air. Yet insanitation still reigned supreme in the physical air. Government action to improve the sanitary state of our towns was for long known to be imminent. When that action came, in 1848, it established Local Boards of Health in many of our towns. Full of the new ideas, and brimming over with enthusiasm, a large number of influential Tauntonians endeavoured, in 1847, to push forward a bill, known as "The Taunton Improvement and Market Bill." A large public meeting on the question was held in the old Assize Hall of the Castle. Many of the Trustees were present. Nevertheless, two months later, they decided to oppose this bill in the House of Lords. Their opposition was successful. The Lords threw out the bill. It was, however, impossible to stem the tide of sanitary reform. There now existed in the town a "Nuisance Committee." Their occupation seems to have been the discovery of all "ancient and fish-like smells," and bringing them to the notice, if not the noses, of the Trustees. This Committee must have been blessed with really good scent. Pigsties, ash-pits, cesspools, uncovered drains were remorselessly tracked down by these worshippers of the goddess Hygiea. The Trustees must have been astounded at what really good noses, working in a righteous cause, could do. The owners of the nuisances were ordered to remove them, and threatened with a fine of ten shillings a day during their continuance. The threat seems to have been effectual.

Though the Trustees had thought it their duty to oppose "the Taunton Improvement and Market Bill," they decided, with the approval of many influential inhabitants, to send to Parliament a bill of their own with the same title, in 1848.

The Public Health Bill, establishing Boards of Health, had just been passed. The Trustees proposed that their bill should include "the importation" of the new Act. The principle of this bill was that the Trustees should cease to be a co-opted, and become an elected body. It may be assumed, that with this modification, they hoped still to govern the town. The "Nuisance Committee" has already been mentioned. There was now in Taunton a Committee, known as "the Health of Towns Act Committee." This Committee strongly objected to the bill proposed by the Trustees on the ground of its cost. They urged too that opposition to it was certain. On the other hand, a largely signed petition was presented to the Trustees in favour of the bill. The necessity of a rate had been recognised by the latter. The conclusion of the petition is interesting and bears on this point, "We beg most earnestly to request you," said the petitioners, "to re-consider the subject of rating with a view of reducing the limit from one shilling and sixpence to one shilling in the pound."

How glad many, on whose backs the ploughers have ploughed long furrows, would be if they could go back to such figures now!

The Trustees' bill was dropped, "it melted into air, into thin air." The Board of Health was established in the town in 1849. There was a kind of marriage between the new Board and the Market Trust. It may be described as, on the whole, a happy marriage—dissolved only by the demise of the Board, when the Trust was re-married, this time to the Corporation. That body will have to deplore the loss of its venerable bride.

Difficult points had to be adjusted : but the Trustees and the Board lived in harmony and at peace with one another.

The first question that rose for settlement was that of lighting the streets. The Board of Health had no wish to be responsible for this expense. The Trustees, on the other hand, had found it more and more difficult to pay for the lighting which had become an ever growing burden on their resources. They were compelled on one occasion to pay a portion of their debts to the Gas Company out of the coppers lying in the Bank, which the Bank had refused to put into account. They owed the Gas Company a large sum. They eventually paid it by borrowing. It is no wonder then that the Trustees wished to get rid of the lighting. Conferences took place between the Board and the Trustees. There were the usual committees, discussions, conversations, deputations, and legal opinions. The Trustees were of opinion, "that they ought to pay their debts before lighting lamps." They declared that they would give the use of all their plant to the Board, if only it would take over the lighting. This friendly dispute went on for some little time, during which the Trustees were still doing the lighting, and not lightening their burdens.

At last, however, the Trustees prevailed, and, in 1850, they were free of a burden which their resources had become unable to meet.

The question of cleansing and watering the town

was as acute as that of lighting it. The Board of Health was no more willing to assume this responsibility than the Trustees were to retain it. The Trust was expending, in 1851, about one hundred and forty pounds yearly on this work, but obtained some relief by a contribution of fifty pounds from the Trustees of the Turnpike roads.

They therefore continued to "cleanse and water" such streets in the town as were "turnpike roads," while the Board of Health was responsible for smaller streets. This dual control lasted until 1854. The Trustees gave a considerable sum towards the new plant required by the Board, as well as an annual payment, ultimately fixed at one hundred and five pounds annually, to that body. The new Board were unable to carry out the work for less than a yearly charge of nearly four hundred pounds.

The Board, which at first had neither cleansing nor lighting to do, must have found occupation in the work of drainage and water supply.

The Taunton Waterworks Company were now supplying water from their new reservoir on the Blackdown Hills, though for years many preferred to drink the contaminated water of the pumps.

The drainage question alone must have given the Board a good deal to think about. We find from a Minute of the Trustees, in 1851, that the Board of Health purchased "Rice's sewer" at a cost of over five hundred pounds. Who Rice was, and where his sewer lay, may possibly be the subject of archæological investigation at a future date.

Dr. Alford has told us that "some of the old drains were found to run uphill." We may be sure that such

THE CENTRE OF THE TOWN AND PARADE, LOOKING NORTH, *circa* 1850.

drains were soon destroyed and replaced by better sewers.

From the year 1854, therefore, the Trustees were more free of burdens, which to a body unable to impose any rates had become insupportable. The care of the Markets and of their property has been their main responsibility since that time.

In 1856 the Trustees, who for some years had been "encompassed with a sea of troubles," were confronted with a fresh difficulty. This was the question of "watching and guarding" the Markets and other property belonging to them. This duty had originally fallen to the lot of the old-fashioned constables. When Sir R. Peel substituted his "new police," Taunton equipped and maintained its own police. The Trustees paid the annual sum of twenty pounds, six shillings, for their services in guarding the Markets. When the town lost its own police, and was dependent on the County police, the Trustees were unable to come to any arrangement with them, or obtain any protection from them.

As, however, we hear nothing more of this sad story, it may be assumed that the arrangements made by the Trustees with their own servants in extension of their duties, and the general superintendence which the police exercised over the whole town, banished all gloomy anticipations.

During the fifties, the Trustees had the usual crop of license questions to deal with. In 1851 an application was made to open a butcher's shop in High Street. The Trustees decided, "that it is not expedient so to do."

In 1856 a leading corn merchant was prosecuted and fined for selling corn in his shop without a license. A little later, however, this peccant corn merchant and others were allowed to sell corn on their premises, on taking out a license.

In 1854 persons hawking fish in the town were prosecuted. One of these dealers could not resist the temptation of calling with fish at "the Salmon Hotel," in East Street. The very name of the hotel was enough to banish any thought of the possible ire of the Trustees. It must have possessed a magnetic attraction to anyone with fish to sell.

The result may have surprised the man who invaded the haunts of the salmon.

The Trustees heard of his crime, and their Clerk was directed to summons T. Smith for his temerity. His was a case of the salmon catching the man, rather than the man the salmon.

## CHAPTER X.

Growing Demand for Shops — Raising of Butchers' Licenses—Eventual Closing of Butchers' Shops—A Determined Butcher who Carries on "War to the Knife"—His Great Stroke Fails—The Trustees and a Hostile Public—"Port after Stormy Seas"—Sale of Fish and Vegetables in Shops—Early Telegrams—Economical Dresses—How to Get Good Bidding—Roof Climbing.

A MARKET was formerly regarded as the principal seat of trade. Here a seller of any commodity would find customers : here a purchaser would find his wants supplied. Shops which, in our early history did not even exist at all, were not rivals with the market for provisions produced in the country, till quite modern times. When the original Market Acts were passed, that was still the current view. This opinion gradually changed. The change was no doubt in part due to the growth of towns, which put more and more people out of easy touch with the Market.

It was much better, so people reasoned, that there should be shops for every kind of food as well as the Market. Why have to walk three-quarters of a mile or so for a bunch of carrots, a pound of pork chops, or a salmon steak ? The Market, it was no doubt asserted, was all very well in its way. It had kept prices normal and gave a housekeeper a pleasing choice of goods, but at a pinch, and when there was no time to lose, the Market was nowhere compared with the shop round the corner. The argument was unanswerable. Shops were a public convenience. People were resolved to have them and to go to them. The Trustees saw that it would never do to defy this sentiment. At the same time, they had to consider the interests of the Market and the maintenance of its revenue. That was also a duty which they owed to the public and themselves.

We have seen that, in the case of butchers and corn merchants, they met the difficulty by allowing the sale of meat and corn in shops, on the payment of annual sums to the Trustees for such licenses. In connection with the butchers and these licenses, serious difficulties arose, owing to the fact, as must be plainly stated, that the Trustees wanted too much for them. Eventually there was a tempest in the town, which almost overwhelmed the Trust.

In 1864, the three butchers' licenses for shops which then existed were raised to fifty pounds each. The three butchers declined to accept the change. The Trustees, on their part, rejected the tenders of the butchers. At length, however, when tenders were again asked for, the three butchers, possibly in fear of tenders from outside butchers, offered no less than seventy-nine pounds each for their licenses. These were to hold good for three years. It was an astounding sum to pay, and the Trustees must have been almost ready to embrace the butchers. When the three years were over, however, the eyes of the Trustees were opened. The same butchers now only offered twenty-six pounds, fourteen shillings each for their licenses. The Trustees seem to have been greatly incensed. They unanimously resolved to close every butcher's shop in the town. One of the butchers was named Hardwill. His name exactly suited him, for he proceeded to defy the Trustees, and sold meat in his shop as usual. He was convicted and fined. He was again convicted and fined. Brought once more before the magistrates, he succeeded in securing an acquittal, owing to the unwillingness of the witnesses against him. He was not a man, to use an old-fashioned expression, to be "overcrowed."

The Trustees, however, were soon up and doing. More actions were brought against Hardwill, and he was convicted and fined on seven different counts. Hardwill was now more than ever determined to avenge himself on the Trustees. They had tried the law on him, and now he would try the law on them. He shrank from no trouble and spared no expense. He applied to the Court of Queen's Bench to issue a mandamus to the Trustees to show cause for their failure to maintain lamps in the streets and to light the town with gas. These duties, it will be recollected, had passed into the hands of the Board of Health by arrangement with the Trustees. The result of the trial must have been a bitter disappointment to Hardwill, who undoubtedly supposed that he had trapped his opponents. The case was heard by a full Court, and the Lord Chief Justice, Sir A. Cockburn, himself presided. Not only did the Court express an unfavourable view of the application and dismiss it, but commended the Trustees for the way in which they had managed their funds.

There is no doubt, however, that the feeling in the town on this question was intensely adverse to the Trustees. They themselves saw that they had gone too far. The resolution which had caused so much trouble was rescinded. The Trustees also expressed their willingness to grant more licenses for the sale of provisions in shops. The Trustees, however, had raised a storm which it was not easy to calm. Largely attended meetings, hostile to the Trust, were held under the superintendence of one of the Bailiffs of the Borough. The Trustees were in effect told that they had reached the state of "the lean and slippered pantaloon," and should quit the stage. The Trustees adopted a conciliatory tone. They declared their readiness to be free of their obligations if more suitable management of their duties could be obtained. "Threatened men live long." The truth of this adage has been proved more than once in the history of the Trust.

The trouble died down. The three butchers consented to pay thirty-five pounds each for their licenses to sell meat in their shops. Each of the butchers was also required, as usual, to take two stalls in the Butchery, on Wednesdays and Saturdays, and one on other weekdays.

It was not until 1862 that any application seems to have been made to the Trustees for the sale of fish and game in shops. In 1865, three licenses were offered at fifteen pounds for each license. Only one of these was accepted by any fishmonger. The first man to sell fish and game on his own premises was Quick, whose reputation as a politician was not forgotten for many years. He it was who stated before the judge who was trying one of the chronic election petitions in Taunton, that "he once voted for the Radicals when they gave him fifty pounds."

Licenses had eventually been given, in 1860, for the sale of fruit and vegetables in shops, after a great deal of haggling between the Trustees and the dealers. The latter were assessed on a scale between ten pounds and five shillings, according to the volume of the business. These assessments were afterwards revised and reduced.

Few persons now living can realise that there was a time when the public did not go to the Post Office to send their telegrams. An examination of the Minutes of the Trustees dispels this illusion. The telegraphic service was originally in the hands of "The Electric and International Telegraph Company." This company, in 1860, decided to move the centre, which they had established at the Taunton Railway Station, and asked for a lease of a portion of the Fish Market, then held in the Corn Exchange. The lease was granted, and the office opened. Here, in an atmosphere redolent of fish, Tauntonians despatched their telegrams for nearly six years. At last, however, the officials objected to the savour of the fish, which was described in plain language, as "an intolerable stench." Fish and telegrams, so long united, parted company. The Minutes of the Trust carry us to the early days of "the Volunteer Rifles," commonly called "the Rifle Corps." Old inhabitants may remember the drab uniform which the Volunteers wore in the sixties. Captain Sanford, son of the Squire of Nynehead Court, applied for the use of "the Butchery," for the drill of the Taunton Company. The request was granted. The Company accordingly drilled in "the Butchery." They had a change of atmosphere for the better when practising with the rifle at the butts in Orchard Woods.

The local Board of Health destroyed a pleasing feature in the town when they diverted the water which, as a few old inhabitants still remember, ran along High Street, East Gate, Fore Street, and North Street, and formed the "rhines" of the town. The Trustees were incessantly asking for an explanation of this unwarrantable alteration from the Board. That body, probably having none to give but love of change, does not seem to have vouchsafed an answer. With the passing of the rhines, the rhine-ridders disappeared from public notice. They still exist, however, in honourable obscurity. They will undoubtedly be found ready to take up their duties as soon as the Corporation restores the rhines.

The Trustees were charitable, but they were also economical. Like Gilpin's wife, they had "a frugal mind." When some "merino curtains" in the Assembly Rooms had become valueless to the Trustees, they were sold to Miss Young, at the easy rate of one shilling. Miss Young undertook to send the curtains "to the needlework classes in Lancashire for making garments for the distressed females there." One would imagine that "the distressed females" must have been more "distressed" than ever, when compelled to assume this vesture.

An instance of sagacity, coupled with generosity, may be noted. The Trustees were quite aware that good bidding for the tolls was more probable if the bidders were in really good humour. They knew too that nothing more stimulates this virtue than "refreshments." They allowed no less than five pounds for these aids to bidding, when the tolls were let in 1861.

A very uncommon complaint was made to the Trustees by the Clerk of the Market in the same year. It appears that the servants of a lady occupying a house which adjoined the present Westminster Bank, were in the habit of sallying from a window and enjoying themselves on the roof of the Victoria Rooms. The Trustees took the view that even the fairy steps of these nymphs might injure the roof. They said nothing about the prospect of harm to the maids themselves. "It is ordered," says the minute, "that the Clerk shall give notice to the lady to discontinue the practice." How the lady could discontinue a practice which she had never begun, is a problem more easily stated than solved.

## CHAPTER XI.

Petitions for a Charter—Inquiry Held—An Eloquent Advocate—An Unusual Hobby—Charter Granted—"Will you step into my Parlour?"—Town Hall Project Started and Dropped—Electric Lighting—Corporation Street—"Bonfire Boys"—New Town Hall Project—Appeal to Charity Commissioners — Taunton Corporation Act — The Trustees Surrender Their Trust—Speech by Mr. G. H. Kite.

FOR some years the question of obtaining a new charter for the Borough had been before the public. There were many who believed that a Mayor and Corporation would confer real benefits on the town. There were others, equally sincere, who apprehended, as a result, heavier rates and more controversy and disputes. There can be no doubt, however, that the change was inevitable, and that if the matter were once seriously taken in hand, resistance would be hopeless. As a climax approached, petitions for and against incorporation were sent to the Privy Council. Among the petitioners against the charter were the Market Trustees.

As a result of these petitions, a Commissioner was sent down, in 1876, to conduct an inquiry and report to the Privy Council. The Commissioner, a former officer in the Army, seemed addicted to an almost Spartan brevity. If, however, he was a silent oracle, the solicitor appearing for the promoters of the charter spoke at great length, with considerable eloquence and sarcasm, and some inaccuracy. He poured ridicule on the Court Leet which appointed the Bailiffs, who convened public meetings and were the returning officers at elections. He made very merry over the Constables' feast, the funds for which he forgot to say were in the main provided at the personal cost of members of the Court Leet. He said much about the natural beauties of the district, and remarked that "the county itself is said to derive its name from the summer-like temperature of the air." He did not give the names of the experts whose derivation of the word "Somerset" he seemed to accept. There was indeed much that was rather interesting than relevant in the advocate's speech.

The principal witness in favour of incorporation said that "the granting of a charter had long been a hobby with him." When success had crowned his efforts, he found a new hobby. That hobby was the Mayoralty itself. The Commissioner showed a great, but not altogether complimentary, desire to leave the town at the earliest possible moment. He had undoubtedly made up his mind that a town of the size and importance of Taunton should be governed by a Mayor and Corporation. On his representations, the Privy Council granted the charter, and the present Town Council began its existence in 1877. Exactly two hundred years before, the second of the three charters held by the town had been granted by Charles II. That charter had been dissolved in 1792. Eighty-five years had now intervened. Taunton had been almost entirely ruled by the Market Trustees until 1849. The Board of Health, which now ceased to exist, had co-operated with the Trustees from that date. The opposition of the Trust to the granting of the charter was undoubtedly due to their apprehension of its extinction by the new Corporation. No secret had been made of the fact that one of the first steps taken by a Town Council would be the acquisition of the possessions and the powers of the Trustees. An invitation from the Town Council was soon received. That invitation was sent to ask the Trustees to allow their Committee to meet the Emergency Committee of the Town Council, "to consider what steps are necessary to acquire the control and transfer to the Council of the Taunton Markets." It was an invitation to the Trust to execute its own death warrant. Such invitations are not usually received with pleasure. The Trustees assented, and the Committees met. The Mayor then proposed, "That the two bodies should unite for the transfer of the Markets." A further conference between the Committees followed, with the result that the Trustees referred the matter to counsel. After obtaining counsel's opinion, they declined the proposal.

The Town Council made another unsuccessful attempt in 1885. Two years later, a fresh opportunity presented itself. The conception of a Town Hall, contrived to seat between two and three thousand people, was held before the minds of the dazzled inhabitants. This was the year of Queen Victoria's Jubilee. What more worthy memorial of this event, it was urged, could be found than the erection of a Town Hall on the site of the old Market House? The public imagination caught fire. Men were then, as they are now, like the Athenians, very much in love with novelty.

A public meeting was held, and a resolution passed

that a joint Committee of Town Councillors and Trustees "should meet to consider the question of building a Town Hall." In the course of the meetings and negotiations which followed, the Town Council once more demanded the surrender of the entire property of the Trust. If that could not be granted, the Trustees were asked to sell the Market House, Arcades and a portion of the Parade, as a site for the Town Hall. These proposals were rejected by the Trust.

Though another large meeting was held in favour of the scheme, it languished and was dropped. Neither Town Council nor Trustees could move alone. A financial tangle existed which nothing but the closest co-operation between the Corporation and the Trustees could possibly unravel.

During the later years of the last century, the Trustees carried on their duties with vigour and success. They consented to the installation of the electric light on the Parade, in 1881, by Massingham. He undertook the installation as an experiment at his own cost. The installation became permanent, and the town itself was soon illuminated in the same way. The Trustees worked in complete harmony with the Town Council when the new road, known as Corporation Street, was made in 1892. They had consented to the sacrifice of some of their property in the construction of this new street. That step was ultimately found unnecessary. The Trustees were thanked by the Town Council for "their co-operation and valuable assistance." A high compliment was paid them for their management of the cattle, sheep and pig markets in 1891. The Government Inspector stated "that he had visited these markets, and that for cleanliness and efficiency there are no better in Somerset." The Trustees never failed to decorate the town on the occasion of any important local event, such as the visit of the Royal Agricultural Society, or the inspection of the Yeomanry by the Duke of Cambridge in 1889. While they rightly resisted the sale of provisions in contravention of the laws of the Trust, they increased the number of butchers' shops, even though this measure involved a loss of revenue. They did their best to keep their buildings in good repair and to adapt them to the altered circumstances of the time. They were not quite so hard on the sportiveness of youth as the Trustees of earlier days. When "the Bonfire boys" applied for permission to keep green the memory of Guy Fawkes, on the 5th November, 1888, by means of a bonfire, tar-barrels and fireworks on the Parade, a benignant assent was given. In 1890, the Trustees removed the flints which then covered the seat of the operations of "the Bonfire boys," and faced the site with asphalte. That improvement cost the "Bonfire boys" their amusement. They probably now imagined that the Trustees had hearts as hard as the flints which they had displaced.

The years slip by, as Horace told us long ago. Ten years had passed since Queen Victoria's first Jubilee. As her second, or Diamond Jubilee approached, the Town Hall scheme came to life again. The Town Council was most anxious that the Town Hall should no longer be but a castle in the air. The principal aim was undoubtedly to alter the dual authority governing the Town, and to relieve the Trustees of their work and responsibilities. This Diamond Jubilee gave the Council its opportunity. If a chance had been missed before, they were resolved that another should be turned to better account. Prompted by the expressed wishes of the Town Council, the Trustees themselves proposed the erection of a Town Hall to commemorate the Jubilee. They were however advised, on the highest legal authority, that no such scheme could be carried out without the consent of the Charity Commissioners. The necessity for this consent lay in the fact that the Trust was ultimately a charitable one. The original Act did indeed state that the property of the Trust was to be held and its tolls collected for the purpose of paying off its debts and borrowed money. When this had been accomplished, the income was to be applied to the education, clothing and apprenticing of children of St. Mary's parish. This the Trustees had never done, because they had always been in debt. This clause in the Act made the assent of the Charity Commissioners necessary, before the Trustees could borrow a large sum for the erection of a Town Hall. The Charity Commissioners were therefore appealed to, and an inquiry held by their representative. The Town Council had by this time discovered fatal objections to the scheme formulated by the Trustees.

Mr. G. H. Kite, one of the Trustees, but acting on this occasion as Town Clerk and representing the Town Council, appeared before the Commissioner and opposed the scheme on their behalf. The Town Clerk raised several objections. He maintained that the Trustees had exhausted all the borrowing powers to which they were entitled, and even if they could and did borrow, such a course would render more distant than ever the control of the town by a single authority.

This single control would then have to wait until the then existing and suggested new debt were liquidated. The Town Clerk also took exception to the plans of the proposed new Town Hall, as the erection of the building would involve the destruction of the existing Market House and Arcades, built in 1772, which were characteristic of the town and had been pronounced on competent authority a good specimen of the architecture of the Georgian period. He said, moreover, that it was unreasonable that a Town Hall should be erected by the Trust, before the ultimate rights of the Corporation and the position of the Charitable Trust had been decided upon. As a result of these arguments, the application of the Trustees for permission to borrow money for the purpose of erecting a Town Hall, was rejected by the Commissioner, with the intimation that no such scheme could be carried through except under a special Act of Parliament.

None the less, negotiations between the Town Council and the Trustees continued, and in 1899 the Corporation proposed going to Parliament upon several matters connected with the town. The two bodies then agreed that this was a good opportunity to settle once and for all their relative positions as regards the Markets. Consequently the Town Clerk accompanied a deputation from the Corporation and the Trustees to interview the Charity Commissioners, who consented to support a clause of extreme importance in the proposed Act. This clause provided that the claim of the Charity Commissioners, on the reversion of the Markets, could be met by the payment of a sum of £500 to be devoted to educational purposes in Taunton. The Commissioners also promised to allow the insertion of clauses in the Act providing for the raising of a loan by the Corporation to enable the Trustees to build a Town Hall, if considered advisable. They also agreed that the property in the Markets should ultimately vest in the Corporation. When the approval of the Commissioners had thus been obtained, the way was clear for action.

As a result, the Taunton Corporation Act, 1890, was brought into being and passed, in 1900, after an examination of the Mayor and Town Clerk by a Committee of the House of Commons. This Act embodied the various clauses agreed upon with the Charity Commissioners.

The statutory power for building a Town Hall was never exercised, as the raising of a large sum of money for the purpose would have prolonged the life of the Trust for a period of 45 years, during which the loan was to be paid off by means of a sinking fund. In addition to this, long before any scheme for building a Town Hall could be carried into effect, all excuse or reason for so great an expense and for the demolition of the old Market House had vanished. The Post Office, which was to have taken over part of the accommodation in the proposed new building, had now a splendid home elsewhere. The Lyceum, which provided ample sitting room for plays, concerts and other entertainments, had been built. The Corporation had obtained a permanent home in the old Grammar School buildings in Corporation Street, and there was a fine equipment of other public buildings in the town. Only a faddist or a crank would any longer dream of searching the pockets of the public for money to be spent on so superfluous a luxury as a Town Hall. As the years sped on, it must have seemed to many that the final settlement between the Town Council and the Trustees would never come. The unexpected, however, often happens. The fateful hour at last struck, and on January 1st, 1926, the Trustees themselves brought the matter to an issue. It was then, that at a meeting of the Trustees, under the chairmanship of Mr. R. Bruford, Mr. G. H. Kite, after due notice, proposed a resolution for the transfer to the Town Council, under the Municipal Corporations Act, of "the rights, powers, estates, property, and liabilities of the Trustees." Four stipulations only were made. Of these one required recognition by the Town Council of the long and valued services of Mr. W. H. Wake, the Clerk to the Trustees. Another demanded the co-option of an agreed number of country Trustees on the Committee for the Management of the Markets for an arranged period. The two other stipulations were equally reasonable and uncontroversial.

Mr. Kite, in moving the resolution, gave a short history of the Trust. He stated that its origin was due to the efforts of patriotic citizens to remedy crying evils existing in the town, and improve the Markets. Reform and progress were the aims of those who financed and piloted the scheme which founded the Trust in 1768. A further object of the promoters had been to assist in the education of poor children of St. Mary's Parish, a charity which might be considered obsolete in these days of free education. Mr. Kite showed how quickly the disreputable inns and erections on the present Parade,

PLAN OF CENTRE OF TAUNTON, 1926.

which were a disgrace to the town, were swept away by the Trustees.

He maintained that if a memorial of the work of the Trustees were sought, one had only to look round and observe the Market House, Arcades and Parade, the Victoria Rooms, the spacious covered Meat Market, and the Corn Exchange, which existed as permanent monuments of the care and thought bestowed upon them.

Mr. Kite pointed out the difficulties which had beset all efforts to transfer the Markets to the Corporation. These difficulties had at last been overcome.

The Trust, said the speaker, was never meant to be permanent. It had most ably discharged its duties, and now it had finished its course. The finances of the Trust could no longer bear the strain which the efficient management of its duties and properties required.

The motion in favour of the transfer was carried by a large majority.

The Town Council, on receiving the proposals of the Trust, unanimously welcomed and accepted them under conditions with which the Trustees unanimously complied. The Market Trust, with its long record of good and faithful service, thus passed into the domain of history. A new chapter in the life of the town was to begin on October 1st, 1926.

# APPENDIX.

1. A List of the Taunton Market Trustees from the creation to the dissolution of the Trust.

2. Copy of Advertisement, 1821, advertising for Tenders for Lighting the Town with Gas.

3. Copy of Advertisement, 1822, as to Orders made by the Trustees.

4. Copy List, about 1820, of Tolls imposed by the Trustees.

5. Copy of Inscription on Sir B. Hammet's Memorial Tablet in Wilton Church.

6. Copy of Inscription on Corner Stone of Victoria Rooms.

A LIST OF THE

# TAUNTON MARKET TRUSTEES

From the Creation to the Dissolution of the Trust.

---

1768.

Sir Thomas Dyke Acland.
Sir Charles Kemys Tynte.
Rev. Thomas Camplin.
John Dyke Acland.
James Bernard.
Arthur Acland.
Coplestone Warre Bampfylde.
John Collins.
Richard Hippesley Cox.
Edward Clarke.
Richard Coombe.
John Frauncеis.
Abraham Gapper.
William Hawker.
John Jeane.
John Lethbridge.
Henry Powell.
Alexander Popham.
John Sanford.
William Sanford.
Robert Ware.
Francis Warre.
Nathaniel Webb.
Isaac Welman.

1769.

Ferdinando Anderdon.
John Affey.
William Bellamy.
James Bindego.
Rev. Malachi Blake.
William Barrow.
William Barrow, Junior.
Samuel Brooks.
John Cabbell.
John Clitsome (Brazier).
John Clitsome (Apothecary).
John Clitsome (Grocer).
Thomas Cogan.
John Coxe.
Richard Daubney.
John Elderton.
Joseph Evatt.
Francis Folaquier.
Francis Folaquier, Junior.
Thomas Foy.
James Foy.
Robert John Foy.
Thomas Gunston.
Thomas Grove.
John Halliday.
Edmund Trowbridge Halliday
Benjamin Hammet.
Thomas Hancock.
John Harcombe.
James Hare.
Ames Hellyear.

EBENEZER JEFFRIES.
JOSEPH JEFFRIES.
JAMES KIRKPATRICK.
JOSEPH LONG.
JOHN LUTLEY.
JOHN MALLACK.
JOSEPH MELHUISH.
JOSEPH METFORD.
JAMES MINIFIE.
THOMAS NEWCOMER.
LUKE NOBLE.
JOHN NORMAN.
JOHN NOWELL.
JAMES PARSONS.
THOMAS PARSONS.
SYDENHAM PEPPIN.
JOSEPH PIKE.
JAMES POOLE.
CHARLES POOLE.
THOMAS POPE.
GEOEGE POPHAM.
JOHN POPHAM.
NEWDIGATE POYNTZ.
SAMUEL REED.
JOHN SHUTE.
GEORGE SKINNER.
JOHN SOUTHEY.
WILLIAM SPILLER.
THOMAS SPILLER.
ROBERT STONE.
WILLIAM STONE.
THOMAS TOWELL.
LUTHER TROTT, Junior.
SAMUEL WATTS.
JOHN WEBB.
JOHN WEEKS.
SIMON WELMAN.
HENRY WHITMARSH.
GEORGE WILLIAMS.
JOHN WESTCOTT.
JOHN WHITMARSH.
JOHN HAMMET.

1781.

HENRY WILLIAM SANFORD.
THOMAS JEANE.
THOMAS SLOCOMBE.
THOMAS DARCH.
ROBERT PROCTOR ANDERDON.
WILLIAM CEELY.
JOHN BURRIDGE.
WILLIAM KNIGHT.
PROCTOR THOMAS.
SAMUEL BROWN.
WILLIAM MILLS.
ROBERT DAW.
HENRY PAUL.
GEORGE LISSANT.
WILLIAM BUNCOMBE.
JACOB TURNER.
WILLIAM TUEXBURY.
REV. PEARD JILLARD.
ROBERT BUNCOMBE.
JAMES SLAPE.
ROGER COLE.
JOHN WARREN.
JAMES BRYANT.
AMBROSE PENNY.
JOHN BUNCOMBE.
JAMES MANLEY.
JOHN BLUETT.
JOHN BADCOCK.
MATTHEW FRANKLIN.
THOMAS COLES.
FRANCIS CAPON.
THOMAS WOODFORD.

James Parsons, Junior.
Samuel Daw.
John Burcher.
John Noble.

1791.

Rev. Dr. Crossman.
John Bult.
Thomas S. Bult.
John Burrow.
John Lethbridge.
Michael Dickson.
Thomas Southwood.
John Burrow.
John Sealey.
Sir Thomas Gunston.
John Cogan.
Malachi Blake, M.D.
Charles Cox.
Thomas Clitsome Coles.
Hugh Payne.
William Bellamy.
John Buncombe.
John Capon.
John Way.
Rev. Joshua Toulmin
James Stowey.
John Shute.
Clitsome Musgrave.
Samuel Sweetland.
Thomas Procktor.
Robert Bindon.
Thomas Foy.
John Hayne Bovet.

1804.

William Cox.
Rev. Buckland Bluett.
William Beadon.
John Clitsome, Junior.
John Pinchard.
William Kinglake.
John Bluett, Junior.
James Melhuish.
Richard Meade.
Charles Poole, Junior.
Clement Drake.
John Gunstone Musgrave.
James Bryant.
Isaac Badcock.
Rev. John Gale.
Ellis Button Mitford, M.D.
John Tyndall Warre.
Rev. Francis Warre.
Robert Buncombe, Junior.
Samuel Hine.
Samuel Norman.
Phillip Doble Burridge.

1816.

Robert Kinglake.
Rev. Francis Hunt Clapp.
Robert Franklin.
Thomas Woodforde, Junior.
John Buncombe.
William Trenchard.
John Vowles.
H. Warren.
Henry James Leigh.
John Poole.
John Liddon.
Joseph Welsh.
Robert Beadon, Junior.
John Cogan, Junior.
Wm. Charles Cox.
James Penny.

JOHN BUNCOMBE CAPON.
SIR. T. BUCKLER LETHBRIDGE, Bt.
HENRY POWELL COLLINS.
CHAS. PROCTOR ANDERDON.
EDWARD JEFFRIES ESDAILE.
HENRY WARRE.

1826.

EDWARD BEADON.
HENRY BADCOCK.
JAMES BUNTER.
RICHARD KING MEADE.
JOHN IVIE.
* WILLIAM PRICE PINCHARD.
GEORGE STONE.
CHARLES WELSH.
DOWNING BLAKE.
WILLIAM BEADON, Junior.
HENRY BUNCOMBE.
THOMAS COGAN TANNER.
REV. THOS. SWEET ESCOTT.
ISAAC DEACON COLES.
JOHN CLITSOME MUSGRAVE.

1832.

JOHN BADCOCK.
WILLIAM BRYANT.
WILLIAM BLATCH COX.
JAMES BILLETT.
HENRY BOWER.
EDMUND TROWBRIDGE HALLIDAY.
ROBERT BADCOCK.
WILLIAM WOODLAND.
JAMES JEBOULT.
JOHN EALES WHITE.
FRANCIS POPHAM.
WEBB STONE.
JOHN ALEXANDER MARTIN.
EDWARD JAMES BUNTER.

1834.

JOSEPH COX.
JOHN HEUDEBOURCK.

1835.

ROBERT ARTHUR KINGLAKE.

1838.

CHARLES NOEL WELMAN.
REV. GEO. ROBT. LAWSON.
JOHN MOCKRIDGE.
JACOB JOGGETT CHAMPANTE.
JAMES VIBART.
REV. HENRY BARKER.
REV. WILLIAM WOOD.
JOHN BILLETT.
WILLIAM EDWARD GILLETT.
CHARLES HARMAN.
CHARLES WOODFORDE KINGLAKE.

1840.

†* VINCENT STUCKEY REYNOLDS.
WM. HENRY BARKER.
WM. HOLE.
FREDERICK REEVES.

1841.

REV. ROBERT SMITH BOWER.
* HENRY CHARLES TRENCHARD. Son of William T
ROBERT BUNTER.

1843.

JOSEPH HITCHCOCK.
ROBERT PARSONS.

1844.

WILLIAM BLAKE.
AMBROSE GODDARD LETHBRIDGE.

* Partner of William Trenchard

†* Nephew of Vincent Stuckey

CAPT. SAML. AMPLIN MELHUISH.
GEORGE STEVENSON.
~~PHILLIP D. HAYMAN.~~
HENRY SWEET.

1845.

REV. DR. COTTLE.

1846.

CHARLES H. HIGGINS.
JAMES TRUDELL.

1847.

THOMAS COKER.

1848.

RICHARD MEADE KING.
JOHN FREDERICK NORMAN.
CHARLES HENRY CORNISH.
DR. FRANCIS HENRY WOODFORDE.
JOHN HAYDN HORSEY.
RICE BLAKE.

1849.

THOMAS RAWLE.
FREDERICK MAY.

1850.

REV. FREDK. JEREMIAH SMITH.
SAMUEL PARSONS.
WILLIAM FRANK ELLIOT.
JOHN LEAKER.
RICHARD CARVER.
DR. REGINALD BURRIDGE.
JOHN ROY ALLEN.
FRANCIS WHEAT NEWTON.
WORTHINGTON COKER.

1851.

JOHN BLUETT.
~~PHILLIP THOS. COGAN.~~
THOMAS BLACKFORD.
† GEORGE TRENCHARD.
REV. HENRY PARR.
WILLIAM RAWLINSON.
CHARLES BAKER.
JOHN WIDGERY STREET.
JAMES BOND COLES.
WILLIAM RICHARD HITCHCOCK.

1852.

JOHN EASTON.
REV. WILLIAM CHAPMAN.
THOMAS PATTON.
†* EDWARD BAGEHOT.
HENRY WARE.
CHARLES LIDDON.
JOHN CHRISTOPHER EASTON.
* FREDK. ALFRED TRENCHARD.
REV. WM. THOS. REDFERN.
ARTHUR CHARLES COX.

1853.

FRANCIS WELSH.
SAMUEL POLLARD.
WILLIAM BLAKE.
WILLIAM BEADON, Junior.
SAMUEL COGAN.
REV. FRANCIS WARRE.

1854.

JOHN WOODLAND.
JOSEPH HENDERSON, Junior.
DR. KINGLAKE.
CHARLES JAMES TURNER.
ABRAHAM TURNER.
JOHN HAMMET BEADON.

* Distant cousin
†* Merchant of brother of Thomas Watson B.

† Banker - manager of Stuckey's Bank in Taunton, leased Shuttern House to Frederick T.

1856.

JOHN STEPHENS.
WILLIAM WOODLAND.
HENRY TURLE.
HENRY ALFORD.
HENRY DANIEL KING.
JOHN PRING.
CAPT. GEORGE BEADON.
RICHARD MEADE KING.

1857.

ROBERT APLIN ENGLAND.
ERNEST ROSSITER.
JAMES SLEE BULT.
THOMAS COGAN.

1858.

RICHARD MEADE KING.
Banker (Stuckey's)

1859.

REV. WM. ARTHUR JONES.
ARTHUR SUTTON.
WALTER PRING.
HENRY HINE BALL.

1860.

+ VINCENT JOHN REYNOLDS.
s/o Vincent Stuckey R

1861.

* BIDDULPH PINCHARD.
DR. KELLY.
REV. JOHN PENDRID SCOTT.
WILLIAM ALLEN.
RICHARD EASTON.
CHARLES GIBBS.

1862.

WILLIAM BISHOP.

1863.

HENRY JAMES ALFORD.
REV. WM. ROBINSON CLARK.
DR. EDWARD LIDDON.
WM. BURGE HELLARD.
EDWARD EASTON.

1864.

EDWARD LYNE PARSONS.
JOHN BIRD.

1865.

HENRY JEFFRIES BADCOCK.
HENRY PRINCE.

1866.

DANIEL BADCOCK.
WALTER MEADE KING
WILLIAM PALMER.

1867.

DR. JAMES HURLEY PRING.
WM. HY. POWELL GORE-LANGTON.

1868.

DR. SAMUEL FARRANT.
HENRY MILLS.

1869.

CHAS. JEFFRIES WATSON ALLEN.
GEORGE GILLETT.

1870.

ARTHUR MALET.
CLITSOME MUSGRAVE.

s/o. Partner Pinchard & Pinchard, solicitors

1871.

THOMAS JAMES SHEPHERD.
WILLIAM STRODE BRAGG.
ROBERT FOURACRE.
DR. HARNESS.
ROBERT BRUFORD.

1872.

HENRY BARKER.
JOHN EDWARDS.
EDWIN BRYANT.
E. DENNING.

1873.

CHARLES PAUL.
WILLIAM BALMAN.
REV. F. HOWSE.
EDWARD RENDELL.
JAMES BOND.

1874.

ROBERT BAILEY.
J. M. FISHER.
J. BARTER.
W. H. HEWETT.

1875.

REGINALD BARNICOTT.
H. J. PENNY.
JOHN DUDER.
J. H. DUNNING.

1876.

COLONEL RAWLINGS.
R. H. SEARS.
G. W. MITCHELL.
W. J. EASTON.

1877.

PETER TAYLOR.
THOMAS KITE.
*GEORGE H. KITE.
THOMAS BOND.

1878.

CAPTAIN TOMLIN.
CAPT. H. B. PATTON.
F. W. NEWTON.
REV. FREDK. J. SMITH.

1879.

JOHN WITHYCOMBE.

1880.

W. S. GIBBS.
ARTHUR STEEVENS.
RICE BLAKE.
JOHN GAY PRICE.

1881.

REV. S. ADAMS.
G. H. GREGORY.
T. CORAM.
R. MATTOCK.

1882.

THOMAS BIFFEN.

1883.

CECIL SMITH.
REV. J. P. HEWETT.
ALEXANDER SOMMERVILLE.
J. H. FARRANT.
C. H. SAMSON.
GEORGE SAUNDERS.
CHARLES COURT.
ALFRED LEWIS.
JOHN HAMMET.

* Solicitor, partner in solicitor's firm either Montague's or Frederick's. Continued Fred's practice after his death. Possibly once Fred's chief clerk.
His son Married Emma Fred's daughter (Aunt Emma)

1884.

W. H. Fowler.
C. H. Sweet.
Jos. Buckland.
*Sidney Redman.
Alfred R. Iles.
Geo. Saunders, Junior.
Major Helyar.
Rev. W. P. Williams.
+ Montague Trenchard.

1885.

F. H. Collier.
Geo. Denham.
S. A. Bragg.
Samuel Fisher.

1886.

Alfred Skinner.
James B. Webber.
Wm. Henry Fisher.

1887.

*Eland Clatworthy.
W. R. Trotman.
*J. G. Vile.
H. Murray Anderdon.
W. H. Tazewell.

1888.

James Dredge.
Thomas Chapman.
Edward Theodore Alms.
Oliver Beadon.

1889.

Robert U. Hartnell.

1890.

Thomas J. Martin.
William H. Westlake.
E. J. Harris.

1891.

William Adams.
Alfred E. Perkins.
H. Harman.

1892.

H. J. Van Trump.
James Scarlett, Junior.
H. Gurnett.
T. G. Williams.
Henry J. Spiller.
Thos. Starkey.
Robt. Mattock.
W. H. Greenham.
Robert Stook.

1893.

*David Brown.
Henry Franklin.
W. C. Fry.
E. Goodman.
Alexander Hammett.
J. Hassall Kirtley.
J. Lock.
William Potter.
Malcolm Glen Ross.
James Stevens.
*F. B. Wickenden.
*Isaac Bryant.
Moses Fardoe.
William Goodland.
R. F. Greenslade.
Charles Harman.

+ Montague s/o Henry bankrupt 1880's

W. KIDNER.
THOMAS LOCK.
WILLIAM OSBORNE.
*H. COZENS.

1894.

EDWIN KIDNER.

1895.

*J. E. KINGSBURY.
W. F. GIBBS.

1896.

E. RISDON.
JOSIAH LEWIS.
WILLIAM PERCY.
*THOMAS COCKS.

1897.

*JOHN WHITE.
MORTIMER PAULL.

1899.

CHARLES LEWIS.
C. PEARD CLARKE.
WILLIAM LOCK.
CHARLES MEDWAY.

1900.

CHARLES HARMAN, Junior.

1901.

WALTER NORMAN.
*HOWARD MAYNARD.
*RICHARD HITCHCOCK.
EUSTACE G. BOULTING.

1902.

W. H. RENDELL.
*SAMUEL KIDNER.
*GEORGE HINTON.
C. MURRAY LEWIS.
*F. W. BAKER.

1903.

GEORGE SPILLER.
*ROBERT BRUFORD.

1904.

*THOMAS HARRIS.
*CHARLES J. BUCKLAND.
J. KIDNER.
*R. C. BERE.

1905.

*CHARLES W. TAVENDER.

1906.

*ALFRED J. BEARE.
*ALFRED E. GOODMAN.
JOHN RENDELL.

1907.

*WILLIAM J. VILLAR.
*SAMUEL J. WRIGHT.

1908.

*PERCY J. BARNICOTT.
GEORGE SCARLETT.
*C. HAROLD GOODLAND.
*CHRISTOPHER NORMAN.

1909.

*Ernest M. Chapman.
*Arthur C. Allen.
*Ernest Saunders.
*Henry Gillham.

1910.

*Henry Powell.
*W. R. J. Greenslade.
*William England.

1912.

W. F. Whittingham.

1913.

† *E. Bagehot Kite.

1914.

*F. S. Arnold.

1915.

E. J. Huddy.
*E. P. Peters.

1916.

H. Chapman.
*F. W. Bond.
*A. C. Mole.
*P. V. Pearse.

1917.

*S. B. White.
*C. W. Stansell.
Wilfred Spiller.
*Thos. Durston.
*R. Richards.

† *E. Bagehot Kite,
*E. Saunders,
*C. H. Goodland,

Re-elected after statutory disqualification for non-attendance during war service.

1918.

*H. C. Colthurst.
*H. S. Hare.

1919.

*T. G. Stone.

1920.

*G. F. Ireland.
*H. Westlake.
*H. Scott.
*J. C. Badcock.
*F. W. Biffen.

1922.

*A. J. Spiller.

1923.

*Percy Clements.
*W. M. Turner.
J. E. Goodland.
*J. Tazewell.

1926.

*G. U. Farrant.
*George West.
*E. J. M. Chapman.

N.B.—The Trustees in 1926 are marked with an asterisk.

† s/o ~~Harry~~ George, the author, husband of Aunt Emma ~~father of Joan & Charles. married Emma T. (Aunt Emma)~~

*COPY of Advertisement, 1821, advertising for Tenders for Lighting the Town with Gas.*

---

## TAUNTON

## GAS LIGHTS.

IN pursuance of the undermentioned Resolution of the TRUSTEES of TAUNTON MARKET, at their Meeting, held the 6th of July instant, I give Notice that I shall be ready to receive Proposals until the 3d of August next, for lighting the Town with GAS, the same to be done at the Risk of the Company, and the Rate of Profit to be limited.

> "RESOLVED, That it is the opinion of this Meeting, that the Town should be Lighted with Gas, and that a Company be formed for that purpose, agreeably to the directions of the Act of Parliament.
>
> "That a Fund be raised by subscription, in Shares, of £50 each, for accomplishing the same, and that no Individual be a Holder of more than one Share, until after the next Meeting of the Trustees.
>
> "That the Public be invited to become Subscribers, and to state the Rate of Profit at which they would form themselves into such Company.
>
> "That the set of such Subscribers to the amount of £4,000, who shall offer the lowest Rate of Profit, shall be accepted by the Trustees, to form the Company, and that the Resolution be advertised in the Felix Farley's *Bristol Journal*, *Birmingham Gazette*, and *Taunton Courier*, once in each."

LETTERS to be free of postage.

R. MARSINGALL,

*Clerk to the Trustees.*

Taunton, July 9th, 1821.

*COPY of Advertisement, 1822, as to Orders made by the Trustees.*

## TAUNTON MARKET,

### 14TH JUNE, 1822.

I GIVE NOTICE that the TRUSTEES have this Day made the following ORDERS or REGULATIONS to commence and take effect on and from the 22d. instant, subject to variations as circumstances may arise :—

1st. That the Corn Market, which has been usually held in the Eastern Arcade, will thenceforth be held and kept on the North Side of the Ground Floor of the New Market House.

2d. That the Granaries or Store Rooms of the New Building be opened for depositing Corn, Grain and Seeds, under the care of a Store Keeper, who is to be sworn and give Security for the faithful discharge of his Duty; the Depositors paying a Half-penny a Bushel, or One-penny a Bag for the first Week, and half that rate per Week for a longer period.

3d. That the Large Room in the New Building be opened from Ten to Four o'Clock, for the Accommodation of all Persons transacting business by Treaty or Sample, but not for the sale of any Articles in gross or bulk; that nothing be taken for such use of the said Room, but that it be, and be called "THE FREE EXCHANGE ROOM."

4th. That the said Large Room may be hired on other Days than Saturdays, for Auctions, Sales and Exhibitions, on such Terms as the Clerk of the Market will communicate.

5th. That all the Branches of the Market be held on the Ground Floor and Area of the New Market Place, on all other Days than Saturdays, so that, from the 22d Instant, nothing be exposed to sale in the Arcades, or on the Parade, except Saturdays.

BY order of the Trustees,

R. MARSINGALL,

*Clerk to the Trustees*

*COPY List, about 1820, of Tolls imposed by the Trustees.*

# A TABLE OF THE TOLLS
## OF
# TAUNTON MARKETS.

## BY ORDER OF THE TRUSTEES.

| | s. | d. |
|---|---|---|
| EVERY Butcher who has a covered Standing on a Saturday, and takes the same by the Year, to pay on every such Day .. .. .. .. .. | 2 | 1 |
| If the Butcher does not take the Standing by the Year, he is to pay on such Saturdays as he shall use the Standing .. .. .. .. .. .. | 2 | 7 |
| Every Butcher who occupies a Standing on any other Day than Saturday, to pay .. .. .. .. | 0 | 9 |
| N.B. No Butcher will be permitted to Under-let his Standing, and if any other Person be found to occupy such Standing, he is to pay for the same as if he occupied any other Standing. | | |
| Bakers, Glovers, Pedlars, Confectioners, Ropers, Hatters, Chandlers, Hosiers, Tobacconists, Shoemakers, and any other Traders who have Standings under the Arcades on Saturdays, to pay each, on that Day .. .. .. .. .. .. | 1 | 1 |
| But any of the above Traders who have not Standings under the Arcades are to pay .. .. .. | 0 | 11 |
| N.B. No Standing to be more than Eight Feet long, without paying for the additional length in proportion. | | |
| Persons selling Fish any Day, having a Standing, to pay .. .. .. .. .. .. .. | 0 | 8 |

| | s. | d. |
|---|---|---|
| And for every Pot of Fish, not having a Standing .. | 0 | 1 |
| Persons selling Cheese to pay per Cwt. .. .. and after the same rate for any additional weight. | 0 | 1 |
| Each Person selling Butter to pay per Basket .. .. | 0 | 1 |
| Each Person selling Earthenware to pay for the use of a Spot of Ground, not exceeding Eight Feet by Three .. .. .. .. .. .. | 1 | 0 |
| And for every additional Square Yard .. .. .. | 0 | 2 |
| Persons selling Brooms to pay, per Dozen .. .. | 0 | 0½ |
| Persons selling Poultry to pay for each Basket, not exceeding Two Feet square .. .. .. and so in proportion for every additional Basket. | 0 | 1 |
| Persons selling Scythes, Hooks, or other edged Tools under the Arcades .. .. .. .. .. | 1 | 1 |
| And for a Standing outside to pay .. .. | 0 | 11 |
| Persons selling Corn, Grain, or Seed of any kind, to pay for each Tub or Vessel .. .. .. | 0 | 1 |
| Persons selling Vegetables, having Stalls provided, to pay by the Week .. .. .. .. .. | 1 | 0 |
| But if they find their own Stalls .. .. .. | 0 | 8 |
| And for any Tub or Basket, in addition to the Stall .. | 0 | 1 |
| Persons having one Tub to pay .. .. .. .. | 0 | 1 |
| But if they occupy Two Yards and the width of a Tub and so on in proportion. | 0 | 2 |

N.B. Any Person or Persons who shall vend or expose to Sale any Corn or Grain, Fish, Meat, Poultry, or other Provisions which are usually sold in public Markets, within any of the public streets of the said Town of Taunton, or within the space of ONE THOUSAND YARDS from the Bounds of the said Market, and shall be convicted thereof, shall, for every such Offence, forfeit and pay the sum of FIVE POUNDS, one Moiety whereof goes to the Informer.

R. MARSINGALL.

*COPY of INSCRIPTION*

*on Tablet in St. George's Church, Wilton, Taunton.*

SACRED TO THE MEMORY OF

SIR BENJAMIN HAMMET, KNIGHT,

LATE AN ALDERMAN OF THE CITY OF LONDON AND IN
FOUR SUCCESSIVE PARLIAMENTS.
ONE OF THE REPRESENTATIVES OF THE TOWN OF TAUNTON.
WHO DEPARTED THIS LIFE ON THE
22ND DAY OF JULY, 1800, AGED 64 YEARS.
HE WAS BLESSED BY NATURE WITH EXCELLENT TALENTS,
A CLEAR AND COMPREHENSIVE MIND,
A FERVID IMAGINATION AND AN ENTERPRISING SPIRIT.
IN PUBLIC LIFE HE WAS EQUALLY DISTINGUISHED FOR HIS LOYALTY, PATRIOTISM, AND TO HIS MUNIFICENCE HIS NATIVE TOWN OF TAUNTON, TO WHICH HE WAS MOST ZEALOUSLY ATTACHED, OWES MANY OF ITS LATE AND GREATEST IMPROVEMENTS.
IN PRIVATE LIFE HE WAS JUST, FAITHFUL, GENEROUS, LIBERAL TO THE POOR, AND A FIRM FRIEND TO INDUSTRIOUS MERIT.
HE LIVED HONOURED AND BELOVED BY HIS FAMILY, AND DIED SINCERELY REGRETTED BY A LARGE CIRCLE OF MOST RESPECTABLE FRIENDS.

## *COPY of INSCRIPTION*

*by Mr. Norris on a brass plate let into the Corner Stone of the new Market House, now the Victoria Rooms.*

HUNC LAPIDEM
FORI RERUM VENALIUM PRIMUM
POSUIT
C. K. K. TYNTE ARM :
SUMMUS LATORUM LIBERALIUM
E PROVINCIA SOMERSETENSI
PRAEFECTUS
PRID : CALEND : MART :
MDCCCXXI
SIT FELIX FAUSTUMQUE.

---

THIS FOUNDATION-STONE OF THE
MARKET HOUSE WAS LAID BY
C. K. K. TYNTE ESQUIRE :
PROVINCIAL GRAND MASTER
FOR THE COUNTY OF SOMERSET,
ON FEBRUARY 28TH, 1821.
"PROSPER THOU OUR HANDIWORK."

Lightning Source UK Ltd.
Milton Keynes UK
UKOW02f1911221216
290694UK00001B/49/P

9 781447 462415